Waiting for the Whistle

A daughter's Memoir of Death, Grief, Gratitude, and Growth

Lynda Ryan

Waiting for the Whistle: A daughter's Memoir of Death, Grief, Gratitude, and Growth.

© Lynda Ryan 2026

ISBN: 978-1-923277-81-6 (paperback)

Published in Australia by Lynda Ryan and InHouse Publishing.
www.inhousepublishing.com.au

A catalogue record for this book is available from the National Library of Australia

Dedicated to Ev, Orla, and Arlyn.
You guys are my happiness, my dream
come trues. I wanna squeeze you so
hard you'll break. You've made me all
that I ever wanted to be; happy, and
a mother. Wanting the best for you
means wanting the best for myself.
Thank you for that clever gift.

My earthside gang members, Samby
and Jude.
I couldn't have asked for a better team
to ride all the steep, windy, winding
cliff-top roads, low-lying flooded
paths, rocky dirt tracks, peaceful and
captivating grassy trails, and long,
straight highways that dying, death,
and grief took us along. Thanks for
sharing all the tears and laughter with
me. I am so grateful for all that both of
you are.

Contents

New Cycles and Old

Eileen McCabe ©
31 December 2008

May your hours be filled with moments when your
life unfolds to show, that the times that you have
come from were the ones you had to know.

As Goodness feels and sees through you, there's
hope for life on Earth. So, living time the way you
do demonstrates your worth.

This road of love brings light and shade where
shadows may conceal; the truth — we're all
connected to the Source of all that's real.

When life throws out each challenge, and you're
not sure where to turn, remember love will light
your way, through trust, the path discerned.

Then days will fill with meaning, as your heart
spills o'er with love. Experience brings wisdom
when the heart and soul are one.

As each day shows its grace to you, the truth will
sometimes hide. But know when angels bless you
that, my love is tucked inside.

Prologue

Eulogy by Samuel Tully
22 January 2021

Eileen Frances McCabe was a storyteller. This is her story.

Born on the 31st of October 1953, she came into this world at Tweed River Hospital, Murwillumbah, northern NSW. The third daughter of Michael and Veronica McCabe, aka Mick and Von, she spent the first two years of her life at the family's house on a share farm in nearby Doon Doon.

In 1955, Mick and Von, along with Eileen and her older sisters, Ann and Michele, moved to Lismore in search of work. After spending the first three months living in a tent, they eventually moved into a house provided by the Department of Housing on Wyrallah Road. Soon after, yet another daughter was born, when Eileen's baby sister Debra came along, making the family a party of six.

In January 1958, the family of four girls was finally joined by a brother when Von gave birth to Michael (Jnr). Soon after this, Eileen began school at Lady of Lourdes Infant School in East Lismore, which she would walk to each day, accompanied by her older sister Michele "Chellie".

In August of that year, the family moved to a new house on Crown Street in South Lismore, just across the road from her Aunty Laine's house. She also moved schools in the process to Our Lady Help of Christians Primary School, just across the creek from the new house.

On New Year's Eve 1960, shortly before midnight, her grandfather (whom she called Dadda), passed away.

Although only a young girl, this was a significant life event and played a big part in forming the strong sense of family and remembering the generations before her that would become such a big part of her life in later years.

In 1965, she began high school at Saint Mary's College for Girls in Lismore, and four years later, after completing 4th form, left school to take up work in the shoe department at AGR's department store in Lismore, then later, for the first of two times, at The Northern Star Newspaper in Lismore, where Mick also worked for many years.

In December 1968, Mick and Von welcomed their sixth child, yet another daughter, as little sister Judith entered the story, and the family was now complete.

In July 1973, at the Italo Club in North Lismore, Eileen met a scruffy-looking gentleman by the name of Ralph. He later tells her that it was actually the third time they'd met; however, she does not recall the previous two encounters. Clearly, they were more memorable for one of them than the other.

In October the following year, on Eileen's 21st birthday, Ralph and Eileen celebrated their engagement, and five months later, on the 29th of March 1975, Eileen and Ralph were married at Our Lady Help of Christians Church in South Lismore. The reception was held at the Italo Club, where they first met ... or at least the first time Eileen remembers meeting anyway. Soon after, they moved to Dubbo, where Ralph was already based for work.

They moved to Toowoomba in 1976, and in January 1977, after a marathon labour and coming perilously close to dying in the process, she became a mother for the first time when daughter Lynda was born at St. Vincent's Hospital in Toowoomba. She now had a family of her own, and the love and nurture required to raise a child was something that came naturally to her, as being a mother was something that she was well-suited to.

In 1979, Eileen, Ralph, and Lynda left their Tor Street home in Toowoomba to move back to the Northern Rivers to start a new business, building squash courts in Casino. In December of that year, she became a mother for the second time, giving birth to a beautiful baby boy called Samuel ...

Or as Mum liked to call me, her favourite child. (She asked me not to tell Lynda that, though, so just keep it under your hat if you would!)

In 1984, she began working for Beauty for All Seasons as a colour consultant, advising people on the best colours to wear to suit their complexion and natural features. In case you were wondering, I'm a summer, hence my choice of attire today (wink at Mum). Thanks, Mum.

In 1985, Eileen and Ralph separated and later divorced, resulting in her spending several years moving between Lismore, Casino, and Byron Bay to be close to us kids before moving to Brisbane in 1989 in search of work. This was a period of great sadness for Mum, as being separated from her children had a devastating impact on her, and she spent the entirety of this time working to reunite with us and bring us back tighter. During this time, she also studied alternative healing, completing diplomas in hypnotherapy and natural healing.

In 1991, she moved back to the Northern Rivers when she was finally reunited with Lynda and I, and the three of us moved into a unit on Rifle Range Road in Wollongbar. Soon after, she would return to work at the "family business" once again, The Northern Star, where her brother Michael and his wife Julie were also working at the time.

In 1992, she experienced her second near-death experience, suffering from a twisted bowel that was a result of complications from the caesarean she underwent while giving birth to Lynda all those years ago. Thankfully, she was rushed to hospital in time to undergo surgery, which saved her life ... and Lynda wonders why I am the favourite child!

As well as nearly dying, in 1992, she began studying at TAFE and, the following year, started a degree in social science at the Southern Cross University in Lismore, graduating six years later.

By 1998, both of us kids had left school and home, and she moved to nearby Federal. That year, suddenly and unexpectedly, her younger brother Michael died at the age of just 40. This loss was something she found particularly difficult to come to terms with, and something that stayed with her right to the end. In 2001, after living back in Lismore for several years, she decided she had had enough of the town and her situation, so she packed up what she could fit in her 1978 Corolla, sold the rest, and set out in search of no place in particular, just a positive change and a new environment.

A diary entry she made on the 12th of July that year says, *"Leaving Lismore. Do not live here again!"* suggests that, at that point in time, she was of the view that the best way to see the sights of Lismore was through the rear-view mirror as you're driving out of town.

She ended up settling in the quiet coastal town of Elliot Heads near Bundaberg, where she enjoyed being near the water and later moved nearby to Alloway on a rural property, where she befriended a stray staffy dog whom she called Gypsy, who would become her dear companion for the remainder of her time there. She was a kind-natured dog who wasn't overly fond of men (except for me) and appeared to have lived a bit of a nomadic life. Gypsy was the kind of dog you got the feeling that, if she could talk, would have some tales to tell. All of this meant that she was a dog Mum found quite easy to relate to.

In 2003, her father, Mick, passed away in Perth, and while not completely unexpected, it was a loss she felt deeply, not just because she'd lost a parent, but also because he was someone she loved and respected deeply. The two of them had a special bond right throughout her life.

After losing her father, her mother, Veronica (Von), made a trip back east from Perth and stayed with Mum at her house at Alloway for about six weeks. This visit was very special to Mum as it gave the two of them the opportunity to spend time together as not just mother and daughter, but woman and woman, and was something they were both very grateful for, and as a result, their bond had never been stronger.

In 2006, she decided it was time to hit the road again, so she left the Bundaberg area and found herself at Greenmount near Toowoomba. This wasn't a place she felt particularly at home, so after a short stay, she moved back to Brisbane and temporarily moved in with Mary, her close friend of many years, before spending several months on the Sunshine Coast looking for a new place to call home.

In 2008, Veronica was nearing the end of her life, so she abandoned this search and took off to Perth to spend her final few months with her mother before she died. Once again, the death of a parent was a great loss for her, but she was comforted by the fact that the two of them had been able to spend time together at both Alloway and in her final months in Perth.

Soon after she returned, in March 2009, an event took place that would transform her life, when she welcomed her first grandchild, a granddaughter called Orla Shae.

The role of grandmother was one that fit her like a glove. She was no ordinary grandmother; she was Mimi, and her abilities to love, care, and support as a mother were matched only by her ability to do all of these things as a grandmother as well.

In 2010, she returned to Brisbane and eventually found herself on the Redcliffe Peninsula. After one false start, she found her unit at Robertson Ave, Margate, where she would live for the remainder of her days. While not necessarily being everything she wanted in a home, she enjoyed being near the water and set about making what was a modest unit into a home where she created her own space and felt comfortable and settled. While she'd always had a keen interest in family history and the importance of remembering the stories and lessons of generations past, it was here that she was able to really develop this passion, as she rolled up her sleeves and set about finding every Jeremiah, Levi, and Hilda Harriet that ever occupied a branch of the McCabe/Collins family tree.

In November 2011, she became a grandmother for the second time when Lynda gave birth to her second daughter, named Arlyn Ivy. Then, five months later, when my partner Kelly gave birth to our first children, twin girls Maeve Lilith and Ada Francesca, in April 2012, her grandchild count now stood at four granddaughters, no grandsons (have you noticed a bit of a common thread in this family?)

Four years later, in June 2016, yet another granddaughter came along when my youngest daughter,

Edith Louella, was born, and the woman they call Mimi now had her five little granddaughters that she loved and cared for more than anything else in the world.

She was a proud participant in not just being a grandmother to the children, but also to their parents, supporting not only with things like child minding so the parents could go to work, but more importantly, providing guidance to Lynda, Ev, Kelly, and I in the qualities needed to be as good of a parent as she had been to her children.

The opportunity this brought, to be a positive influence in the development of her grandchildren, was something she felt proud and privileged to be able to do, and the effect this had can be seen every day in the love they all have for her.

2020 was a year that changed the world, as you may have heard, when a disease by the name of COVID came to town. I wouldn't go as far as to say she enjoyed the COVID-19 pandemic, as the gravity of the impact it had on the world was something that troubled her like the rest of us, but the sense of togetherness, stories of people helping complete strangers in need, and community mindedness that came about as a result was a shift in the world that she took great joy in seeing. She was seeing the world in a more positive light and was very optimistic about its future. Not just for the short term, but the world she would eventually leave behind for her granddaughters as they grow and become older.

Sadly, she didn't live to see how that part of the story pans out because, as we know, after suffering a stroke at her unit in Margate, she died a few days later, surrounded by love, respect, and laughter in the Redcliffe Hospital.

While she would have loved to have been around to see what happens next in the story, the genealogist and storyteller in her would know that a person's life is not the beginning and the end of a story. They are chapters in the bigger story of the world, and what you do with your chapters will influence that story in the generations to come.

When I was a kid, she would regularly say to me, *"Actions speak louder than words,"* and of course, like any self-respecting teenager; I would roll my eyes and think, *Righto, Mum.* But as it turns out, she was actually right (as she was in many other cases I never gave her credit for). Her actions as a mother and woman have had an impact on all of us.

Don't get me wrong, she was fond of a few words, they are pretty meaningful too, most of them ... but it's her actions that will leave the most lasting impression on me.

She was a bloody top mum who gave unconditional love and respect to Lynda and me, no matter what. I hope that I, as a father, have the courage to give my kids the freedom she gave us in growing up to learn my own lessons, form my own views, and even give a bit of cheek from time to time ... just not too much though, eh, girls.

Chapter 1 – Eileen

I'd like you to meet my mum. I can't introduce her to anyone new anymore, so I'm turning this into an opportunity to do so as best as I can, and although this book is about her death, in essence, it's about her life, so it's a logical place to start.

One of the first words that comes to mind when I think of her is "sensitive". She knew that, and it used to annoy her. Not because she didn't agree with it, but because she felt that it limited my awareness of the very resilient and capable parts of her that co-existed with her sensitivity. For too long in my life, I saw her as "too emotional," and because of that, I'll admit, at times I thought she was weak.

Thankfully, I had started to see her more clearly, as more multidimensional, before her death. The beginnings of that shift started around the time I turned 40. I started understanding that her softness in no way diminished her strength, and although you will go on to read about how our relationship continues to evolve despite her death, it's hard to reconcile that her death was the main catalyst for me genuinely prioritising our relationship and learning more about her.

She knew that would cause me regret; she told me so, not that I was listening properly, but it went something along the lines of *"Don't wait until I am dead to put the effort into me."* Yet here I find myself. But, if I focus on the positives, which fortunately I have learnt to do, even though I would not choose to do it in this unique way, her death doesn't extinguish my ability to get to know her better, and in doing so, analyse and get to know myself better, too. So, these days, the word I would use to describe her would be "Magical". A "real" person, in the sense that she wasn't perfect, but she was grounded, had depth, and wasn't interested in being anyone other than who she was. She was introverted and modest, but in no way did that mean that she let people shit on her. She was a sensitive woman, rightly so, because that's where her kindness came from. A strong, confident, quick-witted, and *magical* woman. I am very pleased to introduce you to my magical mother, Eileen, whom I miss every day.

***

Before Mum was "Mum", she was Eileen McCabe. A girl from Lismore who grew up quietly. A "good girl", to her own detriment. A girl who would have loved to have taken more risks and done things that seemed "impossible". She had an adventurous spirit within her compliant exterior. She often felt overpowered by people who could express themselves more loudly, but this didn't diminish her deep sense of self.

Perhaps because she didn't feel she could express herself outwardly, this created more room for internal dialogue and reflection. She had many stories from her childhood that illustrated what a deep thinker she always was, and what a brave and determined nature she had, despite her shyness. She was someone who would have liked to have given more things a go, but because she was a good girl; a result of both her family dynamics and growing up in an era where children didn't challenge authority as much, she went on to become a young woman who not only did what was expected, but more so "did what she was told".

She would've liked to become an archaeologist, a fairy tale crazy idea for a "job", especially for a woman. A young woman from a working-class family, in regional northern NSW in the late 1960s and early 70s, wouldn't necessarily finish high school, let alone even attempt to achieve a dream as irrational as that.

So, maybe instead, she could travel. She liked the idea of getting a motorbike or even going overseas! No, that wasn't realistic either. She'd need money, let alone the fact that a girl in her late teens or early 20s can't just head off into the wide blue yonder by herself, doing something as dangerous and silly as that. Even her attempt at being brave enough to go against the grain by encouraging her younger sister to join her didn't solve that problem.

So, she got a job, something that did provide her with a sense of freedom and pride, to a point. She met a young man. She fell in love. She got married. They moved to a few different towns before settling within an easy driving distance from her hometown to start a business. She had two children and, in doing so, finally found the sense of purpose she needed whilst making her way along the path she was directed to travel on. She put her head down and focused, trying not to turn her head towards the road less travelled, or even to look too far ahead of where she was on any given day.

The little girl with the big imagination grew into a woman who was a very proud mother. Proud of her children, but also proud of herself.

The marriage she thought she'd built her life on ended when she was in her early 30s, resulting in her being separated from her children, her life's biggest heartbreak. Despite the devastation this caused her, she moved forward, trying new things, expanding her experiences and giving her best shot at finding her place in a world that so often seemed to respond by saying she didn't fit anywhere.

She had some wins and some losses. She often felt shattered, but as must be done, she resiliently continued along the winding road of her life's path, always with humility, kindness, and humour. She navigated motherhood from the time of her children's conception until her untimely death with such a beautiful mix of fierce strength and gentle tenderness. She was deliberate with her lessons; an excellent role model. She loved those children to the very core of every little last skerrick of who they were. And later, when she became a grandmother, she leaned in hard with her soft, gentle love for her granddaughters and all four of their parents.

She was a loyal daughter, sister, friend, and wife. She did want more for herself, but focused on what she had, rather than what she did not and made peace with that contentment.

Eileen was a person who showed interest in people and encouraged individuality. She didn't once deliberately intimidate anyone, ever. She took her time, hated being rushed. She forgave but wasn't silly enough to forget. Others may have responded differently to the close-minded responses she got when it came to her dreams. She knew she should be "allowed" to take more control over her life's course, but she wasn't burdened by resentment, and she never ever turned her back on her family.

She understood that when the people she loved boxed her in, it came from a place of both love and fear, so she made peace with it as best as she could and instead developed a deep belief that family is everything. Family connections, whether it be the newest baby joining the clan or someone she'd never met from hundreds of years ago, became a driving force that motivated her to go forward when at times she felt like stopping. She made people feel seen. The lucky few who knew her very well felt that way without a doubt, even if that meant the parts they'd rather not look at. She offered insight into both the shiny and rough parts of the people she loved, but always with a positive purpose. For those who knew her less intimately, she left her mark by always offering kindness, being direct, open-minded, and down to earth, rather than through wild or interesting antics or specific memories of things she did.

She loved me hard, even when I was at my worst. Eileen was a free-thinking, deep-thinking woman; a mother I will be forever grateful for. Choosing her as my own was one of the best choices I'll ever make. I am so proud to be able to introduce you to her and share some of her magic with you.

Please know, as you read on, that ours is a complex relationship and at times it was strained because we are very different and yet very similar. Despite and because of that, we share an extremely close connection without a drop of pretence between us. We disagreed, had outright screaming matches at times, but we also shared a wicked sense of humour and would talk for hours and hours. We knew each other's soft spaces and sharp corners and *always* loved each other deeply.

A lot of what I know about her as a person stems from knowing her perhaps more narrowly as my mum. I helped shape that version of her, and sometimes it's hard to disassociate who a person truly is with the impact or the responses they have to life events. I am sure that some of what I knew to be "her" was influenced by me taking her for granted, being selfish, and needlessly guarded. Although I don't let that eat me up, I feel it's important that I take ownership of that at this early point because she didn't raise me that way. I know it was due to immaturity and normal mother-daughter dynamics to some extent, but she raised me gently, with full knowledge that I could always trust her, but also to both respect and appreciate her. She was no doormat.

Healthy mother-daughter relationships are fed by acknowledging each other's strengths rather than existing on a one-way street that attends only to the child's needs and wishes. She taught me that, however, I wish I had shown her more while she was here, that I got that message, because then some of my experience of knowing her would be clearer, and I would be more comfortable introducing her without premising with that.

While I am clarifying things at this early point, it must also be said, that like Mum, I have what is known as a "dark sense of humour". I prefer the terminology of "sicko", but either one is fine. As this is my first attempt at writing, I can only hope that it translates as you read on, rather than making me and my family seem like heartless psychos.

BEFORE

Chapter 2 – Floating

I have always been "highly strung". My mind so often steers me down a path of worst-case scenarios, and for as long as I can remember, anxiety has always been there, sticking its nose into my otherwise sharp common sense and intuition.

When I called Mum after work on Tuesday to see if she was free to meet for lunch the following week, she didn't answer, but no big deal. I had been meaning to call her the day before, but didn't get around to it, or if I'm honest, couldn't be bothered.

Lying in bed that night, I realised I hadn't heard back from her, which I thought was a bit odd, but for some reason, my brain, which would normally be starting to race into an overdrive of worry at that time of night, told me it was okay. It was too late now. I'd just call her in the morning.

Forgetting to do so until that afternoon, she still didn't answer my call or the two text messages I sent shortly afterwards. Starting to panic, I told myself that it was just my stupid glass-half-empty mind up to its tricks. Everything was probably fine, as it always is. But I couldn't settle with that thought; my racing heart had entered the equation by then, so I decided to call my brother Sam to hopefully offload some of my stress onto him. He has a good knack for almost dismissing my anxiety in a way that usually takes the edge off, so this was a strategy I had used before, but as he lived closer to Mum, I knew he would agree to go and check on her.

He was his usual composed self when I explained the situation, but said he'd head over shortly, once he'd finished work. Luckily, it was the summer holidays, so he could go straight there rather than having to collect the girls from school first.

It is a well-known fact that I am Mum's favourite child (or perhaps a well-used family joke that differs depending on who is telling the story), but despite me being her favourite, it has to be said that he has always been a beautiful son. He has always been very protective of Mum, so my strategy worked, and I felt some comfort in having his cool head on board with a plan.

In the meantime, he suggested I call the fish and chip shop next door to Mum's unit to see if they could provide any clues. Great idea.

A very young-sounding girl answered. I explained the situation calmly, but made it clear I was concerned. Unable to convince myself I was overreacting, I took her welfare into account, so rather than asking her to knock on Mum's door, I politely asked if she would walk up the driveway to check if the car was in the carport. She begrudgingly agreed, returning only moments later to say she couldn't see a green car. I called Sam with this news. By this time, he'd had more time to worry, but he was also on the way there. He asked for a full account of the phone conversation and as a result, was unconvinced she had walked far enough up the driveway to clearly see the car. He said he would call them again with a more direct approach of instructions, calling me back shortly after to say the girl had now reported that the car was in fact there.

So the initial slight sense of relief I felt from the car not being there possibly being because she was out somewhere, was busy and didn't hear her phone, or had left it at home and had just forgotten to call me back, had then merged in my mind to thinking she was perhaps trapped, in pain, or dead after having a car accident on a remote road, or maybe she had been assaulted, killed, or left for dead somewhere, then spiralled into realising that the car being there obviously meant that she *was* in the house, possibly, probably, laying there dead, or at best, injured.

That was how my brain has always worked. Leaping from reasonable thinking to catastrophic in the next second. It felt as though there was no other plausible reason she wouldn't be answering her phone, despite the fact that, I reminded myself, this situation had happened once or twice before, and none of those outcomes had ever come close to eventuating. So indeed, there could be many straightforward reasons.

I was spinning as I did my best to grip onto that knowledge, battling my lifetime tendency of diving into pointless and distressing assumptions. Sam would be there soon. All I could do was wait, the imagery of so many scenarios running wild and vividly through my head.

Panicked, I figured I should practice what I preach when I try to teach my girls to implement strategies such as distraction to combat worry, so I decided to go to the gym as planned. At that time, I was a bit of a gym junkie (or perhaps that's just another one of those well-used family jokes). Sam wouldn't arrive at Mum's for about half an hour, so what good would it do sitting around, losing my mind, when maybe she just hadn't charged her phone or had it turned down or something.

Desperately clinging to that notion, I tried to channel my distress into being pissed off with myself that despite talking about it numerous times, we had never gotten around to putting an emergency plan in place for a 67-year-old woman living alone, with numerous health problems. I knew that at least this "lesson" would mean we'd finally rectify that.

Surprisingly, my distraction strategy worked, but when my gym class finished, and I saw several missed calls from Sam, but no voicemail to say everything was fine, I snapped into instant terror mode. Despite the loud noise in the gym, I rang him straight away, almost knocking people over as I darted around them to get outside so I could hear him.

He said he had found Mum on the floor.

She was being taken to hospital, and he was following the ambulance.

Once outside, I could hear how shaken he was, but I distinctly remember him talking in a deliberately slow voice, as though he was a bad actor pretending to be composed. I remember looking at the speedometer sitting on 75 as I drove through the suburban streets, thankfully only five minutes from home. Leaving the engine running, I ran inside to my completely unsuspecting family.

Failing my attempt to impersonate the same calm person Sam had tried to be, I yelled, "Get in the car right now. Mimi has had a fall. We need to get to the hospital RIGHT NOW."

Within five minutes, we were in the car, my husband Ev driving while I sat in the back to comfort our two girls, Orla and Aryln, for the 50-minute trip. They were understandably frazzled, which I felt guilty for causing, but to be able to touch them and play the role of concerned mother instead of freaking out daughter gave me something to focus on, grounding me as much as possible.

I rang my friend Trish from work, giving her a brief rundown, telling her I wasn't sure if I would be in the next day. Seems funny now that I thought maybe I would be...

Once I finally made it to the emergency department entrance, not the main entrance where I initially wasted precious time looking for where to go, I was met on the footpath by my Aunty Judi.

Judi (known as Jude) is eight years older than me, so she's always been more like a cousin. She is Mum's youngest and closest sister and also happens to be a nurse. I'd made the decision in the car not to call Sam again. I knew he would have enough on his plate, and if I couldn't control the external situation, I figured I could keep a lid on the stress while we made what felt like an excruciatingly long journey there.

Jude and I hugged in silence before I pulled away to ask what had happened. Her face was totally distraught. A bolt of fear painfully surged into every part of my body, bringing with it an awareness that, despite my normal pessimistic outlook, this was actually crunch time for the first time in my life. Somehow, deep down, I knew that this was a totally different ball game. I was so used to expecting but not experiencing the worst. In that moment, it was being served right up under my nose, yet I couldn't comprehend the reality. I remember so clearly the strange mixture of messy confusion and total bolt-upright clarity.

Time.
Stood.
Still.

As I stood wavering between those two "worlds", Jude said Mum had suffered a massive stroke. That was the first of many times the word "massive" would be used.

As we drew each other close for another hug, squeezing my eyes closed in a vain attempt to avoid the scary scene unfolding around me, I asked if Mum was going to be alright. Jude started to answer, but I felt her change her mind and instead breathe in, slowly breathe out, and say nothing. Despite how fuzzy yet zapping everything felt, I had total clarity that this was a pivotal point in my life. Without knowing any of what was to come, I knew my life had changed forever. I could feel it in my bones. A clarity I wouldn't feel or even contemplate again for another few days from that precise moment.

Desperate for more information, I deliberately stayed holding myself up in the hug so I could physically get my bearings, focusing on my legs not buckling as I mentally prepared myself to open my eyes to "check back in to the real world". Rigidly vertical, feeling as though I was levitating upwards, I prepared with a deep breath before pulling away to look at Jude, but before I spoke, her face was saying "No."

"Let's go inside and talk to the doctor".

I am certain Jude would have been reassuring me, trying her best to balance staying calm with honesty, but I wasn't clear if Mum was dead, about to die any minute, or if Jude's reluctance to elaborate was based on the likelihood that Mum had a really tough recovery ahead. Despite the adrenaline that had been pumping through me since talking to Sam outside the gym, amplified by my interaction with Jude, it felt like everything was in slow motion. My brain felt fried. Each piece of information felt like a part of a puzzle that was trying to form a picture in my mind. My brain was overloading in a dismal attempt to protect me from allowing the picture to fully form.

I had been training for this moment my whole blessed, yet panic-ridden life, but somehow, my mind was holding tight and was almost winning the battle with my trembling body. Strange, given that in my entire life, where nothing as significant as this has ever happened, I have *never* felt that removed from the anxiety of emotionally difficult situations. We walked inside. Everything was surreal, even the waiting room seemed fake, too bright, like a movie set.

The next thing I realised was a clue, was that Jude was taking me to "the family room". I know this room from the practical component of my social work studies in my uni days. It's the little room they provide for people who have something so serious going on that they can't just be left in the main emergency area with the less hard-core situation waiters. I baulked; my legs stopped me at the door, thoughts racing through my head. Jude's face, now this room, maybe she is actually dead? Maybe Jude doesn't even know; she just died then, whilst we were outside. Of course, she was dead! How could I be so stupid? Angry that by contemplating anything else, I had set myself up for such an obvious fall, I forced my legs to move me in.

I hugged Sam, who was sitting alone.

He told me Mum was alive.

I don't remember if I asked. I know I didn't ask him anything more.

That was all I wanted to know. My overflowing brain was at capacity. Ev and our girls arrived after parking the car. We all sat quietly, in shock. A volunteer came in, looking for coffee cups. She was smiling, but also had a solemness to her, respectfully putting aside her "just-another-shift" attitude because she was in the "family room", realising that whatever was going on for these people deserved a pull back on too much cheerfulness. Then a nurse came in and told Sam and me we could go through.

He and Jude had already seen Mum but had come back to wait for me, so he led the way while I slowly followed. Mum was down the end of the building in a big open space, all by herself. She didn't look good, but she didn't look that bad either. There was no blood, which made me realise I had been expecting a bloodied body type of situation. She looked tired, and white, and old. She had a slight "stroke" face. That was what was making her look old.

I nervously touched her hand and then held it in mine. It was heavy.

A dead weight.

Floating, I didn't cry.

I felt blocked, like I couldn't feel my feelings properly, and was awkward, as if I was meeting someone new, so I just stood there holding her hand. Then I could smell her. She smelt very strongly of urine — old, acidic, pungent urine that I now know was a combination of urine and faeces, that she had been lying in for days. I could almost taste it in the back of my throat. This was a helpful thing because it pulled me down from my floating feeling, back into reality.

Dazed, but increasingly adjusting to being able to stand on my jelly-filled legs, eventually I said something like

"Hi, Mum. It's me, Lynda."

She didn't respond in any way. She seemed unconscious rather than just asleep. I ran my fingers over her cold, heavy, smelly hand. Her hand, her soft hand. Her hands that had been so busy. Her familiar hands that I knew so well because she always said they were like mine, putting them next to mine to compare and prove her case, while I disagreed. Her hand was now in mine, and I distinctly remember thinking, *I am right, there's no similarity between them, what is she on about with that?* Clearly, some of my normal responses to things were still working sharply.

Eventually, the first of the beautiful, caring nurses whom I remember thinking, *I will never forget her name*, started attending to Mum and introduced herself. I don't remember her name, but she mentioned the smell and said that she had tried her best to clean Mum up, but they don't have the capacity to do personal care in the emergency department. I did wonder if what she meant was that there wasn't much point because she'll be dead soon.

Sam sat, and I stood next to Mum. After a while of us staring at her, Sam went somewhere, and it was just Mum and me. I know I was talking to her, filling in the awkward silence, but I can't remember what I said. I guess I told her how sorry I was that this had happened and was happening, and that we didn't help her sooner. I felt so out of my body, but at the same time, so pressured within it. I know I told my Mum that I loved her during that time alone, but it felt a bit forced, like a token gesture to say at such a time. I hardly ever told her I loved her for some fucking stupid reason, but I'll probably get into some of that later.

A doctor arrived and used the word "massive" again. He mentioned a possible heart attack, which was news to me. He said no one would ever know exactly how long she had been on the floor, which was the main thing I wanted to know. They had only been able to run some basic tests, so he wasn't able to give us an actual diagnosis or concrete prognosis, but he didn't seem overly positive about Mum's long — or even short-term future prospects.

He asked what we wanted done if she needed to be revived or put on a ventilator. Despite its obvious absence, that's when I noticed she wasn't on one. All that time, it had just seemed like a breathing machine type of situation. She was just lying there, motionless, with her hair whiter than I'd ever seen it, a drip in her soft, pale arm, a stiff crisp white sheet over the rest of her body; in this bright white room with its intense, blinding white lights beaming down on her. Sam and I looked at each other, stunned. I was so affronted by his question, despite the care and professionalism with which it was asked.

I felt like saying, "Our Mum is right there, looking like that. She has just been found on her kitchen floor after nobody will apparently ever know how many days of lying there, in the January heat, and now you're asking her kids to decide something like that! That is not a question you should be asking kids! Surely that is obvious! Her parents aren't here, but that's their job, or someone more appropriate, a grown-up at least. Anyone, not us, we're just kids. Wait until she wakes up and ask her. Who are you? Why would you ask us that, you arsehole?"

I forced myself to snap into some semblance of reality so I could answer while still trying to piece it all together. There was no blood, no ventilator; she just looked white, heavy, older, and tired. But we were being asked if we wanted to give her a chance? A chance makes it seem like the choice is clear between two things, life and death, which it was, but it was far more complex than just that. We had to make a choice that could lead to an outcome we had no certainty about. Quality of living. Just being about life and death almost seemed easier.

The situation was so fresh, and we had such limited information. The doctor did at least rule out that she would ever be able to function fully independently. Miracles happen, but we weren't in that headspace. We were clinging to any "facts" he could offer, so if that was the case, it wasn't necessarily the end of the world. She could be perfectly happy; great things may still be to come for her, for all of us, as a result of caring for her. Blessings come disguised all the time. We may miss an opportunity if we don't give her that chance, be brave, take that risk and look after her so well that it pays off. She was young, still so much life to live, and we would make sure she was so happy we didn't give up on her. But to what extent would she need our help?

What if she were completely bedridden, unable to talk, shower, or feed herself? We knew we couldn't ask for her to be revived and then change our minds if the outcome was too distressing or too much to manage, or worse, that *she* would be wishing we had made a different choice. Looking at her, it was easy to visualise her having to live a life void of joy or dignity. That in itself felt unbearable, but that weight was compounded by the fact that our answer, our decision on whether to keep her alive, could result in taking her freedom and happiness away.

She was lying there. Breathing unassisted. Living. But essentially, we had to say whether we thought it was better if she lived or died, which required assessing all of the bigger picture parts that both of those puzzles involved.

A few hours ago, none of this was real. I was just at work. It had been real for *her* then, though. She had been lying there then, too. She had clearly made it through whatever she had been going through for who knows how long all on her own and now we have finally come to help her, but we have to say that if she couldn't keep being so brave, so strong, and so beautiful on her own, that we thought it was best that she isn't given any more chances.

So that's what we said, not in those words though obviously. We both knew that was the right answer; she would have said that too, but I felt as though I was just pretending I knew how to make such an overwhelmingly grown-up decision. Me, the one who had never listened to her, had always thought I knew best or more than her, who always had an answer back, just wanted Mum to wake up and tell the doctor what to do and save us from making a mistake. This question was too hard. It wasn't right that she couldn't speak for herself; that we were forced to pretend to be a big girl and boy who knew the answer.

I was still floating.

From here, my memory gets sketchier. Although I believe that "timing is everything", that concept annoys me now and to some extent, I wish I hadn't just gone with the flow of my grief so naturally in those months afterwards. I wish I had considered this idea and acted sooner to record all the details of this special time in my life, in our lives, because already I'm worried that I can't remember everything, but now is better than never. Through the writing process itself and the eventual record of it, I will forever be able to cling to the moment-to-moment details, so rich with diversity. All the turmoil and intensity. All of the humour and epiphanies. She would see me doing this as part of her legacy to future generations. The next family researcher may find it of some use or interest, hopefully, and it might make it harder for her life to be forgotten.

Processing this way and sharing it makes her life feel more meaningful, like her death was not in vain. She died, there's the spoiler, but that is not the important part; the important part is that she lived. The story of her death will also translate in part as the story of her life.

Mum is the star of this show. Like her ancestors, Annie Hart and Hilda Sargent were to her; she will be my muse. My love for her is the reason that her death meant so much to me. Her death brought me closer to the realisation that her life meant so much to me. A realisation I wasn't living with in the way that it now serves and guides me. So, I want to record it all. I have a compulsion to do so. I know that calling is coming from both of us. The memories of that time and the intensity that came after need to be recorded.

It was my favourite week. That seems strange I guess, hopefully that will make more sense as I go on, but despite my life where I have been so supported, where things have both just fallen into place for me and been orchestrated by me in a way that I have always felt both blessed and proud of, those few days were not just pivotal, but also a beautiful, pain-filled pleasure. And I miss being immersed in that experience, almost as much as I miss her.

At some stage, Ev, the girls, and Jude went home, and much later, Sam and I were told we had to leave too. I had a strange willingness to do so that Sam didn't. His plan was to sit next to her all night, but we were told she was being taken to the ward and were advised to get some sleep. Tomorrow was going to be a big day. I, of course, thought, *But what if she dies?*, but I felt comfortable with the doctor's reassurance that she was likely to remain stable in the short term. I knew at least trying to rest would be important for what was ahead, assuming the next day would likely be a long day of waiting, being bombarded with information, and having to make more decisions, in which case we may regret staying even if we were allowed to stay.

I especially didn't want to be sleep deprived and knew I needed to regain some strength if what we were facing was her dying. Sam went along with it only because he wasn't given a choice. He really didn't want to leave his mummy's side while she clearly needed him so much. We asked if we should bring back her CPAP machine because she couldn't sleep well without it. I see the doctor now through the lens of hindsight, shaking his head in a way that I could have taken insight from, but wasn't yet able to. So, we said our weird goodbyes, with a desperate "see you tomorrow".

Strange now when I think of it. I would have had an overwhelming awareness that this, in fact, could be the "last goodbye", the last time I would see her alive, but I can't remember the details, aside from watching on as the gentle orderly wheeled her down the corridor, off into the more dimly lit unknown.

Sam suggested we should first go to Mum's to clean up. Because of the heat and not wanting to leave the hospital for the foreseeable future, he knew from being there that afternoon that it needed to be attended to.

It was a strange feeling walking up Mum's steps in the stillness of the darkness, imagining her being stretchered down them by the ambos. Sam was visibly shaken by being back there. For him, it must have felt like a lifetime ago, rather than six or seven hours.

We stood together in her kitchen, looking at the spot Sam said he'd found her, while he gave me a brief overview. He'd come up the front stairs, the door was open, and he thought he could hear her, but the screen was locked. He couldn't see around the corner into the unit, so somehow, in a feat of superhuman power, he balanced on the steep balustrade and climbed through her high and tiny bedroom window at the top of the back steps to get in. She had mustered more energy to call for him while he was doing so, quietly saying his name, so he knew she was alive.

He found her lying on the kitchen floor, about a meter from the front door, semi-clothed, semi-conscious. She'd been incontinent, and it was obvious to him that she'd been there long enough that she was in a very bad way. He explained how he crouched on his knees, and she had looked right into him with such relief in her eyes and, I know without being there or him saying so, with such love.

We mopped and tidied up the packets and medical paraphernalia left behind by the ambos. We needed to mop a couple of times to get rid of the smell and make her home her home again, not some traumatic crime scene. We found "evidence" that perhaps she was making lunch at the time it had happened, given the stale, sweaty cheese and pita bread on the bench and brown, squashed avocado on the floor that she must have rolled on. That was the first of our "detective" work.

Sam said that she was dressed in clothes rather than pyjamas, although she had half undressed herself at some point, most likely due to the heat, and to get herself out of her dirty clothes. The lounge room fan was on, but would not have kept her cool where she was, but at least air was circulating, and the screen door was allowing air in. The lights were off, so it must have happened sometime before dark. We grabbed a few things for her, trying not to focus on how alone and scared, uncomfortable, desperate, in pain, sick, hot, and thirsty she must have been, and headed back out into the quiet night air.

In the calm of the dark early morning, we drove across town towards Sam's place, stopping for my first drive-thru Maccas in years on the way. It felt like a strange little treat, like we were on a road trip together again, like we used to do when we were in our 20s, when we'd drive from Brisbane to visit Mum in Bundaberg. There were very few cars on the road; it felt like just us, in our own little bubble.

We discussed how we could arrange her care, who she would live with and the logistics of her going between both of us. We also discussed all potential scenarios, including whether it would be better or not, if Mum pulled through. Driving through Brisbane in the early hours of a Thursday morning, eating Maccas with Sam, talking about Mum living or dying, was immensely surreal.

We arrived at Sam's quiet house and had a quick chat with his partner, Kel. She lent me some pyjamas, and I had a shower. She also lent me some of her undies, and I remember thinking how nice it was to be so comfortable with someone that you can borrow their undies, but also that it's not a regular thing to do, so it reinforced the overall weirdness of the situation. With my niece relegated to her parents' bed for the night and finally feeling clean and refreshed after the physical and emotional workouts I had done, I hopped into bed, surrounded by teddy bears and fairy lights, eventually crying myself to sleep, wondering as I drifted off if when I woke up, my mummy would be dead.

Chapter 3 – Reality

We woke to no news, which we took to mean only that she was still alive, which was at least a relief that she hadn't died alone. I obviously knew the importance of that even then, but not how I understand the gravity of it, for everyone's sake now. Before we left the night before, the doctor said we could return before visiting hours. The seriousness of our reality still hadn't landed in me because I remember thinking how nice that was of him. He must have really liked us or felt especially sorry for Mum to be giving us special treatment.

We didn't race to get dressed and leave in a mad rush, innately knowing we needed to set ourselves up calmly for the emotionally draining day ahead. After a coffee and some toast, the time zone difference meant we were able to call Mum's best friend, Mary, who lives in Germany. Their friendship was very important to Mum, and so too for us. We wanted to give Mary the respect of being included in what was happening as early as possible. It was a very difficult conversation. We didn't want to upset or worry her and weren't entirely sure to what extent she needed to be upset or worried.

As we drove to the hospital, I made arrangements for the girls to be looked after so that Ev could get some hours in at work. As we pulled into the car park, Sam's phone rang. It was Jude. She had just gotten off the phone to a doctor. Obviously through an assumption that had been made the night before, she was listed as Mum's oldest child (which has now become yet another of those well-used family jokes). He called to advise her that Mum would soon be moved off the ward, to the palliative care unit.

My recollection is that we both responded to this news with an amazing sense of calm. We were more than likely also freaking out, but at least we knew what we were dealing with right off the bat. We had just been discussing how it would be a whole day of waiting around for tests and probably no conclusive answers. Yet even before arriving, we were being told that Mum was going to die. It doesn't get much more conclusive than that. We went up the lift in a state of reserved shock, walking quickly to her room. There she lay, looking very uncomfortable, stiff, and white. Her face was slack. We realised she was awake — conscious I guess you'd call it, but her eyes were closed. A nurse named Lena was with her. Sam and I noticed her name badge straight away because Lena was a nickname given to Mum by her dad, our "Dadda". We sat down and told Mum the nurse's name, and she gave a little sideways smile, just like Dadda's smile in fact, now that I think of it, and we shared this nice little "sign" together.

Sam had brought along his Bluetooth speaker. Regardless of what the day had in store for us, we knew we would need music as a coping tool while we waited, to provide a soundtrack of this significant time in our lives and, without discussing it, something special to play as she died if that were to happen, which we now knew would be the case.

Without a clue what we were doing because we'd never been with anyone while they died, we figured we'd better get proceedings underway. Although we didn't know how much time we had, we'd watched plenty of movies, so we assumed we wouldn't have long. Our main objective was to make her feel safe and loved, and playing music is one of the main ways we do that in our family. Returning after being called away from Mum for a brief conversation with a young male doctor who was very insensitive to both our situation and limited medical knowledge, we asked Mum if she wanted some music on; an almost rhetorical question considering we assumed the answer would be yes. I'm not sure how she communicated it, whether she shook her head or grunted, but it was a definite "*No.*" We were surprised but figured we'd let her get away with this clearly poor decision, despite her imminent death. It was her death after all, and if that's how it was to be, too bad for our best laid plans, I suppose.

Sam and I shared an unspoken assumption that the way it would unfold was with us, now thankfully by her side, listening to the music she loved, and that it would all be over in the next half an hour or so. She had made it this far; surely, she couldn't have much left in the tank. I figured we wouldn't even make it to palliative care, despite having no idea where that was. Things always take ages to happen in hospitals, so we would be stuck waiting for a while, and while we did, she would peacefully die. Sadly, and surprisingly, without music, but she wasn't alone, so that was the main thing.

"Obviously", she'd waited for us so she could "slip away" with us holding her hands, just like the movies. We hoped Jude would make it, but we felt no pressure for Mum to prolong things any longer. She had held on long enough. She could go now, suffer no more.

During the consultation with the annoying doctor in the corridor, we were uneasy leaving her side. What was this guy thinking? He knows she's dying; he might make us miss it! She is dying. Today. We knew that now. This was actually what was happening. No need for tests or waiting. Surely, she knew that too? Strange that she didn't want music on? Maybe she *was* waiting for Jude.

Sitting either side of her and talking to make sure she knew we were there, we quickly realised that it's very hard to talk to someone who can't speak, especially when that someone is my mum, who was extremely talkative. When you're caring for someone, you ask a lot of questions. There is nothing else going on in your life worth waffling on about; all you want to know is if they are okay, which requires feedback.

It was evident that she could not only hear but also understand us, but she couldn't speak, and that was how we were used to communicating, naturally. We found ourselves asking her open-ended questions, then quickly counteracting doing so by answering for her, giving her little time to respond anyway, bombarding her with questions and options we could see were frustrating and confusing for her. I didn't feel like I was doing a good job of helping her at all. We managed to slow things down, but she still didn't seem to need anything. She didn't want a drink; she didn't even want her lips moistened. Why? She must be so thirsty; her lips were dry. She didn't want music on when we checked again in case she had realised the error of her ways. I mean, the woman was dying. Surely, she wanted something! What we were offering was basic, very doable, and we so desperately wanted to make sure she was comfortable, happy even? I felt so small and more of a hindrance than anything.

On reflection, I needed her to do it the way *I* needed her to do it, but I didn't know what that was, aside from for her to sit up, open her eyes and be able to say a few words at least. I needed assurance that she was comfortable, that she was okay, despite the "fact" that she would be dead "any minute". I needed to know that she wasn't scared or sad. The thought of her dying like that was breaking my heart more than the thought of her dying itself. I wasn't in any way contemplating what it was going to mean to live without her. I just wanted her to tell me she was at peace, but she couldn't do that for me, or for herself.

At the time, she seemed unable to do anything, but comparatively, her ability to communicate that day was very good. She could move her head. She could lift one arm, hold our hand with that one hand, lift her leg, move her body to shift slightly, and make little groany noises. While we sat there, waiting for her to die, she did try to speak. She tried to say one word but kept stuttering it. We were trying to guess it, throwing words at her. Could it be this? Could it mean that? She was getting frustrated, and we were getting so anxious and sad watching her not being able to get that one fucking word out. Maybe she was asking for help. Man, I wished then that we knew what it was, and desperately still now wish that I could remember even what sound she was making. I'd take that. I would love to know even a silly, pointless thing, like if it started with M or maybe it was a

B? Her last word. Her last word that didn't ever make it to being a word. As I write that, though, I realise we do know what that was. She had called for Sam. I find that more beautiful than I can adequately express. That relationship and that interaction had resulted in her last word.

"Sam."

Surprisingly, and what seemed suddenly, we were on the move to the palliative care unit. Mum had her eyes closed but was still awake, and we had complete certainty by now that she was totally mentally there. Despite how unsettling it was seeing her in the state she was in the night before, we were relieved that at least before losing consciousness, she was aware she'd been found. Now that she was cognisant again, I was worried she might be scared, but be unable to express that. The mere idea of that was a heavy combination of feeling as though I was a small child again, needing my mother, my anchor, to be secure, whilst also wanting to be strong and reassure her. After being on a drip overnight, she was basically her again, although a very sick version of her, but strangely, given where we were off to, she seemed to be on the mend.

The stroke, the *massive* stroke, had somehow not affected her brain's ability to think or understand. Travelling alongside her as she was wheeled along in the clunky hospital bed, I was worried that the noise and lights in her face and the bumpy movements going up and down in the lifts would be jarring to her. She seemed so delicate, and I wanted to shield her. I desperately wanted to make sure she wasn't frightened; it was a bigger concern for me than where we were heading. The hospital was undergoing renovations, too, which made for a longer, even busier, noisier trip than it would have been otherwise.

I don't know if we told her where we were going, it would have been as weird as our "see you later" conversation the night before — something like, "It's okay Mum, don't worry, we're just off to palliative care."

Our best intentions would be to keep her informed, but the fact that I can't remember that very important conversation, one that would have been had with such intensity and considered word choices, tells me that it didn't happen. Not because we were trying to hide anything or patronise her, but an attempt to help her feel calm.

We, of course, believed that she deserved to know what was happening, especially considering how clearly she was comprehending everything. Maybe we expected that she would die before we would get a chance, or we thought it was pointless to tell someone they're dying right before they died, or perhaps we assumed she already knew?

Whatever the case, in our effort to make her feel safe, I now realise that we didn't, at any point, have a discussion with her about the fact that she was going to die. She couldn't ask us, and we didn't tell her. I'm so regretful about that. We didn't do it on purpose, but we really got that part wrong. Everything was happening so quickly that morning, but we didn't see any of the openings we had as an opportunity to do so.

The trip between the two buildings took us outside for a brief moment. Walking behind her, I bent down to tell her we were outside, as if she couldn't figure that out for herself (my concept of what she needed to be told was obviously skewed) and commented how nice it must be for her to have some fresh air and warm sun on her face after all the time she'd spent inside. That one minute along that pathway would be the last time she was ever outside. I vividly remember realising that. I wonder if she did too.

The first thing I noticed about the palliative care unit was a large, framed astrology chart on the wall. It looked a bit out of place amongst all the butterflies and serene sea scenery style pics you'd expect to find in such a setting. I was surprised and happy to see it there, given Mum's passion for all things astrological, and acknowledged it as yet another "sign", another little nod from the universe.

Shortly after arriving, we were met by a beautiful man whom I again thought I would never forget his name, but have. He was very short, fined boned, and very well groomed. He was like a leprechaun, not only because of his bright clothing and stature, but the way he spoke, both in accent and pitch, was just like a leprechaun!

We instantly liked him; he immediately made us feel important. Nothing would be too much trouble. We should ask for help without hesitation; no question would be a silly one. I felt like he genuinely cared about us; it was irrelevant that he didn't know us. He was a wonderful mix of flamboyance and practicality, endearing himself to us as being a bit of a larrikin, while still being deeply respectful of Mum and the situation we were in, easing my fear. The perfect man for that job, and for us to meet right in that moment. He made it seem like what was to come was all going to be okay, even though what was to come was that my mum was going to die. Mum would have really liked him. Jude wasn't there for that greeting, so when she arrived, we told her to keep an eye out for a leprechaun; she would know exactly who we meant.

Soon after the leprechaun left, a nurse asked if we wanted a priest to read Mum her Last Rites. The shock of being asked this was soon overtaken with the heavy realisation that we had yet another important decision to make, and no confidence in providing an answer. Sharing an unspoken sense of urgency, as though Mum was "on deaths door", we didn't feel we should hesitate by having a well-considered discussion, so after a quick chat about the pros and cons, we declined. Although Mum was raised Catholic, she was by no means the practising variety, so we guessed she would think it was unnecessary. Jude arrived shortly after, and we relayed this discussion and our decision to her. Jude agreed that Mum wouldn't feel strongly either way, but she felt it would help Mum honour how she was raised. Her relationship to Mum in that space was insightful and therefore valuable in making this decision. She felt that it was important that Mum share the family tradition of being blessed by a priest before heading off on her journey, and through taking that short amount of extra time to discuss it, and having Judes support and guidance, we knew Mum would agree. Sam raced off to tell someone we had changed our minds. We "knew" every second could be Mum's last, as we waited impatiently, regularly glancing towards the door for the priest to arrive.

Now I can see the bigger picture, as I sit here remembering the course of these events, again I wonder, *why didn't we ask Mum?* It's so clear that all that we needed to do was ask her. Perhaps we didn't consider doing so because we'd taken on the decision-making duties the night before, or were so fixated on our self-imposed, perceived lack of time and assumed we would get it all wrong, after our dismal attempt at communicating with her on the ward. Possibly, subconsciously, we *did* know that we hadn't discussed her prognosis with her directly, which blocked us from asking such a question.

On reflection, I see that although we thought we were being open with her, we were not. Our primary focus was to do everything in our power to protect *her*, but possibly because of fear, we were unintentionally protecting *ourselves* as well.

Asking her what she wanted would require telling her she was going to die, and it seems we weren't emotionally capable of doing that. We also saw her as being terribly sick and didn't fully understand how capable she still was. Also, there was a timing aspect. The course of events until this point seemed strangely to be working in our favour. We got to her before she died on the floor. We'd made it back to the hospital before she died. Yet the speed of our day of waiting on tests, so suddenly turning into the day Mum was going to die, and our assumption that Mum was always only moments away from death, meant that time, every second of time, was of the essence, panicking and distracting us from thinking with this retrospective logic.

We were still motivated by and therefore operating on thought processes, yet to morph into functioning on a different plane, where we were guided by emotions rather than cognition. Things seemed to be happening at high speed, but that was okay, because we were somehow managing to fit everything in and not piss fart about wasting any of the precious time we had left. There were boxes to tick.

Make sure she wasn't alone — tick. Try to make her feel safe — tick. Call the rest of the family to get here — tick.

In the days that followed, the stages of the process and events within the big event would be referred to by Sam, Jude, and I as "the modules". We assigned random numbers for each one as we moved through them, learning as we went. Module 6.75 "How to organise a kick arse funeral", for example. This was one of our first modules after all, we'd only just started our course, and in retrospect, it was perhaps module 1.12 — "Take the time to tell the dying person, if you can, that they are dying, rather than assuming they know or hoping they will guess".

I realise how trivial I'm making it sound, but it kills me imagining Mum lying there, not being sure what was happening. She knew she was in hospital, and knew more than we did what she had gone through to necessitate her being there, but did she know she was dying that day?

Well, actually, she seemed to know more than us that she wasn't dying "that day", but did she know that she was deemed as palliative that day?

Oh, how I wish I could ask her and tell her how sorry I am for getting that bit wrong. We owed her that honesty. We were given no directive by anyone about it, and regardless of the fact that I know she doesn't hold it against me, I wish that I could have opened my heart with her through that conversation when she was "awake", and I still had the chance.

I can't explain why that is so important, why I am filled with so much regret about it, probably because it was a missed opportunity to say a proper thank you to her. To be the one to gently tell her she was dying, whether she knew it already or not, seems like it would be a beautiful way of expressing my love for her, but I wasn't capable of doing so. I was very different before I had the gifts she would go on to give me over the next few days, weeks, and months. There were so many more modules still to get through.

Upon receiving the news in the car park that Mum was going to die, I called Ev in a panic, telling him to leave work, collect the girls, and get back to Brisbane ASAP. Everyone arrived in quick succession after Jude, Ev, Orla, and Arlyn, as well as Kel, my nieces, identical twins Maeve and Ada, and Edith (whose bed I had woken up in), along with Kel's mum, Debby, who had coincidentally arrived at Sam and Kel's that morning for a pre-planned visit for a few days.

I watched the reactions as all the girls saw Mum for the first time, like she was. They were all overwhelmed.

Orla, the oldest, was reserved, as is her way, but wasn't awkward. Crying softly, she went straight to Mum and was a lot more solid than I had prejudged she might be. Our younger daughter, Arlyn, was less of a surprise, diving straight in to talk to Mum and shower her with affection, despite being very distressed and checking for reassurance from me that she was doing the right thing. Sam and Kel's girls had made cards adorned with drawings of hearts and flowers that read things like "Get well soon, Mimi". Edie was very upset seeing her Mimi, whom she loved so much. It would have been so scary for her, and she cried and kept her distance for most of the day. The main thing that surprised me was that none of the girls reacted to the smell of Mum; it was still very strong, but they were so gentle, so loving, and didn't seem bothered, puzzled, or even notice it.

Kel had so thoughtfully brought with her a heart made of rose quartz, and as she gave it to Mum, she whispered some kindness into her ear. Rose quartz, representing universal love, was Mum's favourite crystal. The heart was smooth and solid. It fit perfectly in the palm of Mum's hand, and it was obvious she was very grateful for it. She would have been thinking what a kind and very "Kelish" thing it was of her to do, something simple that could've easily been overlooked, but Kelly had thought to bring it for Mum to have with her at this very important time in her life, when she would need all her strength and the feeling of love to guide her on her way. Mum stroked it in her palm with her fingers. She seemed to be using it almost as an "anchor". Rubbing it, gripping it, turning it, and caressing it.

The priest finally arrived and briefly introduced himself as he approached Mum, and with what felt like no lead-up, he commenced his little ceremony. Up until this, we had been happy when things were actioned promptly, but instantly, this development felt wrong. I sensed an overwhelming foreboding, and it quickly became clear that Mum was very disturbed, but the priest didn't pick up on this. In his defence, he had not been part of the story until this very minute, so he had no reference point; however, Mum was obviously communicating that she wanted him to stop, but obliviously, he kept going with his spiel. I moved closer to Mum, motioning to him to help make that clearer, but again, he wasn't picking up what we were putting down. Thankfully, the Last Rites doesn't go on for as long as most Catholic things do (I suppose that's because time is not always a luxury to be afforded), so once he'd finished, we quickly thanked him and ushered him away.

Our initial assumption was that Mum's reaction was because she didn't want to be sent packing by a priest talking about things that didn't align with her core beliefs, and that she was essentially trying to say, "I'm not a practising Catholic, this doesn't represent who I am, this is not for me!"

I have since come to the belief that her distress stemmed from something much bigger, and as mentioned, this is the part of her dying story that holds the most immense regret in me.

We certainly didn't do everything during those few days perfectly. We did our best, and even this for its time, was us doing so, but it without doubt, really upset Mum, and that means that we really upset Mum. We were constantly worrying that she might be scared, and surely she was when she lay alone on her hard floor, but since being found, scared was only with any certainty our feeling, until, without warning, a priest was standing over her, reading her the Last Rites. I feel no doubt that partly her reaction was shock, but worse, disregard. She had finally been rescued, but suddenly, whether she knew she was dying or not, she was being given her marching orders. Her response was likely a mixture of emotions, but I now believe the main one was anger, and what she was trying to say was:

"No!"

"My time is not up!"

"Please don't give up yet, I am not ready!"

"I have so much left to do, for myself, and for all of you. Don't take that control away from me!"

With all of our judgments and decisions, it's now clear that she knew much more than we did. We would come to learn that she did indeed have so much left to do, and if she wasn't aware until the priest's visit that she was dying, he couldn't have been further from the right person to deliver that news, let alone finding out in such a direct and impersonal way. I obviously don't know her exact thought process, but her response was intense. Having that news sprung on her while the people she loved gutlessly watched on, is hard for me to bear.

Of all the unknowns, and despite knowing that she understands and forgives us, the idea that she felt betrayed is heartbreaking. Even with all the crazy poltergeist shit that was yet to come, I wish I could take that part of the story out. I wish we had taken the time to gently tell her that we were in palliative care and ask her if she wanted a priest to come and do his thing.

That's really all it would've taken — Module 1.12.

Once he left, we consoled Mum and tried to erase what had happened as best as we could, apologising for something we didn't fully comprehend, but knew was our mistake. I recognised that we needed to stop rushing. Jobs had been done. Our family was together.

We needed to just "be".

Love her.

Wait.

With things settled, I realised I needed to call Dad to provide an update, after having only spoken to him once since everything had happened the day before. Mum and Dad had been divorced for over 30 years. Their relationship was not necessarily ongoing, aside from sharing a family, I guess, and increasingly harmonious Christmas get-togethers over more recent years, but we knew he would be worrying, and at least now we had something to update him with, as he wasn't aware of Mum's diagnosis.

Dad took the news with utter devastation. It felt like he was jumping down the phone with shock and distress, and it was evident that he wasn't just concerned for Sam and I; he seemed upset for himself and for Mum. He insisted on meeting us at the hospital; he seemed to be starting the engine before I had even finished my sentence to say there was no need. After living interstate from each other all my adult life, Dad had only recently bought a house down the road from ours, so, having no idea of how things would unfold, and considering he was coming anyway, I asked him to collect a few things for the girls, considering they had left in such a rush again. I knew their coping ability would be better if they had a few of their important things, so I really appreciated his help.

The last thing he stressed before I hung up was, "Tell your mother 'I'm sorry'. Tell her I'm so sorry for everything I ever did to her."

Hearing this blew my mind. I was totally, utterly, stunned and am sure even the look on my face would have demonstrated that as I almost did a little jig with amazement on Mum's behalf.

Without going into the ins and outs of their marriage, divorce, or all the years in between and since, this was beyond unexpected and thrilling to me, but more to the point, I knew this piece of news would be momentous to Mum. She would be thinking it was typical of him to say such a thing as she lay on her deathbed, but that's better late than never. I hurried Dad off the phone to get back to Mum before it was, in fact, too late, again.

Any time I left her side, I was worried she might die, even though in retrospect, most of her faculties were still strong. Despite being able to hear, comprehend, and communicate, in an attempt to make sure she was understanding, I had been repeating everything everyone was saying to her. At one point, she let me know with no doubt how annoying this was, grunting and nodding at me as if exasperatedly saying, "I know, Lynd. I'm not deaf, you know!"

Racing back in, I leaned in close to her ear, not necessarily because it was a secret I was sharing, but I felt it was a private moment for Mum, and in some ways, for Mum, Sam, and me, as we had all lived through many hard years that so often come with the territory of divorce and custody battles. I told her that I had just spoken to Dad, he was very distressed to hear what was happening, and he wanted to apologise to her, emphasising his exact words as I expressed my shock and happiness to her.

"I'm so sorry for everything I have ever done."

Despite the gravity of this very serious moment, we shared a little chuckle, and I'm smiling now, remembering

Mum smirking and rolling her eyes in her head as I caressed her face and shoulders. She had a definite look of satisfaction, but more so relief. An expression that told me she felt vindicated, but not in a smug or arrogant way. After how things had been all those years and in more recent times, she did, in the end, get the apology she always knew she deserved and, in fact, had somehow always known would eventually come. She had a look of grace.

I know Dad's apology was deeply meaningful to her despite its timing and possibly because it was delivered by me. It was certainly something she had needed to hear for the longest time. Although maybe not perfect in every sense, the genuine way it was almost unconsidered, or "blurted out" by Dad, and that she was unable to verbally respond or discuss it, meant that she had no choice but to let it settle in her, perhaps making it more meaningful. In that way, it *was* perfect. She did get this moment, after all the years that she suffered such unnecessary sadness.

At some stage that morning, my cousin and his family, who live near the hospital, arrived to say goodbye to Mum. It was the first time in many years I had seen him, and his partner had made a care package of treats and things for the kids to do, a beautiful and humbling way to meet her.

We also met Bruce, the man in the bed across from Mum. He was dying, presumably of course, but able to sit up, talk, and walk with assistance from the visitors he had on and off throughout the day. I wondered how long he had been there, or been dying for, for that matter.

Now, when I think of it, he had been dying his whole life, no different to anyone. I was acutely aware of his relatively good health compared to Mum and was uncomfortable for almost shoving in his face what his life might look like in the expected and not too distant future. I wondered if watching Mum and us throughout the day was making him anxious or depressed, assuming that he would be feeling at least one of those negative emotions. Dying was such a new and foreign concept to me then. I wonder now, though, even when he had no one by his side, just families in the room, strangers like us, if what he was feeling was peace. Hopefully, he was able to feel the offshoots of all that love, and maybe that, along with the paths he had already taken to arrive where he was, meant that he had a sense of calm about what was to come. Mum would have taken an interest in getting to know him if she could have. He was her last hospital "room-mate". She had had many over the years with her various admissions, often sharing a little story about their lives with me and a rating of how good or bad they were to share a room with. She would have rated Bruce quite highly.

Dad arrived about an hour after I'd spoken to him, rushing in like a bull at a gate. As is his Leo way, he was most concerned that she knew he was there and kept asking her, "Do you know I'm here, Eils?", as if it was a pact that he had promised and wanted her to be sure he hadn't broken. He held her hand, which looked bizarre, but the way he did so seemed to contrast with the soft and gentle approach we had. He didn't do anything wrong, but I was sensitive to the way he was grabbing it too tightly and patting it too hard for my liking. His presence felt a bit jarring, making me feel protective of her. He didn't seem to fit, which, to be blunt, makes sense; he didn't, although his connection to her seemed so strong, I wonder now if he felt he did. To consider that he felt he needed to be there for his own reasons, for our family reasons, and maybe even that she needed him to be there, all of which was probably true, I find both odd and comforting. My world of Mum, Sam, and our extended family on Mum's side was separate for many more years than when they were married, and the dynamic resulting from Dad being there made that very evident.

Dad, on the scene, made me aware that I knew Mum so well. I knew what she would be feeling. I knew that she was very happy about his message; it had been received with gratitude, but she had every right to feel as though it was owed to her. She appreciated and was okay with him being there, but this was her moment, and *our* moment, and at this point, it had nothing to do with him. I knew she would certainly expect him to help Sam and me with arrangements for the kids, put himself out if needed, and make things as easy on us as possible. That aside, for the next part of the journey we were on together and individually, a quick visit was sufficient. Once he'd checked in with Mum, shown his support and calmed down somewhat, we encouraged him to mingle, and he gave us the space with Mum we needed.

Every moment of time was consumed by awareness that Mum would die. That was what we were gathered for after all. It was a constant, "any-moment-now" expectation, with no conscious realisation of the fact that we clearly weren't on the precipice we thought we were.

Throughout the activity of the day, Mum held her rose quartz, and it was on her stomach while she slept. She was clearly grateful to have it, but she would hand it to me when she needed a rest; even the simple task of maintaining a grip seemed to drain her. This going-between-our-hands thing had happened many times throughout the day, but as I handed it back to her on one of these occasions, she gave it straight back to me, quite definitely grabbing my arm, placing it in my palm and closing my fingers around it. It seemed as though she was giving it to me, telling me not to give it back and as she caressed my fist, I had a very clear realisation that while she was awake and strong enough, she had been "charging" it. Throughout the action and when the quiet moments were being shared, she was putting her last remaining energy into that crystal and without words, it was very clear to me that she was giving me something powerful and magical and wanted to make sure that I understood that.

I know my mum. I know she purposefully filled that crystal with love for me, but as her energy drained, it was time to give it to me while she was still able to get that message to me. She gave me her heart, given to her by her other "daughter", Kel, who she also loved, and she knew Kel wouldn't mind. The perfect physical expression of her last gift — a heart-shaped symbol of unconditional love. Something solid and beautiful that I can hold and never forget how that feels.

It was such a blessing that, despite how sick she was, Mum knew we were there for her and that she could still communicate with us. Not only had she not died alone on the floor, but she was able to be a force in the process we were sharing.

Aside from the "priest incident", she was able to maintain a degree of control when her life had so often left her feeling the opposite. I can't say with certainty that this day was the one she needed us *the most* because I assume there were many days when I was too busy or not prioritising her when she needed me, but this surely had to be in her top five at least. The people she loved the most were all there for her, and she knew that. The kids were so well behaved as they went about their day with a beautiful mix of sensitivity to the situation, whilst innocently enjoying their day together, doing things like picking daisies they probably shouldn't have been picking from the garden and placing them on Mum beside the handmade cards.

At one point, when Mum was nicely "decorated", Arlyn gathered the girls around Mum's bed. The four little girls, all under the age of 12, held hands under Arlyn's instructions, while Edie sat on her mummy's knee at the back of the room quietly crying. Arlyn announced that they were creating what she called a "circle of love".

She told them to say or imagine their greatest wishes for Mimi, to send her off with love. As if leading by example, she told Mum how much she loved her and would miss her. She spoke of how lucky Mimi was to be going to see her mum, dad and her brother, "Uncle Michael". Despite having never met them, Arlyn "knew" these important people in her family. She told Mum that actually she "had it pretty good", not only was she going to find out what happens when you die, but she would be with people she loved, whom she hadn't seen in such a long time.

One by one, the others all expressed their wishes for Mum through this sacred demonstration of love. They weren't as vocal, or "familiar" with this process as Arlyn somehow seemed to be, but their powerful love together as a team in that moment was resolute. I'm sure Mum felt the reverence and depth of their feelings. It was so strong you could almost see their connection forming a blanket over her body with their little arms around her. She would have been so proud. It would have been a very special part of the process for her, as it was for all witnessing it, and for the girls both as a group and individually, for their processing and grieving.

Despite this beautiful moment, among others, and the relief that not only had everyone made it not just in the nick of time, but we were able to share so much time together, it had been a long day, so by late afternoon, it was evident it was time for everyone to head off. Ev had a work deadline due, and the girls were all getting tired. It was decided that they would stay in Brisbane, considering I would be going back to Sam's "in a few hours" myself, once Mum died; now that she'd completed her own "goodbye module".

Dad offered to take some of the girls as Kel's car wouldn't fit everyone, and we started organising the kids to head off. There were so many tears from the girls. So much love was showered on Mum. She was such a beautiful grandmother who had intentionally developed a unique relationship with each one of them, so she deserved nothing less. I was so proud and so impressed by how well they expressed themselves, leaving Mum with no doubt how much she meant to them. My two wouldn't leave. They kept walking out only to return for another hug of me, or Mum, anxiously wanting reassurance that I was going to be okay without them. After this had happened several times, with Dad waiting awkwardly in the corridor, unsure of how to "round them up" at such a fragile time, I had to get cranky with Arlyn to get her to go. Although necessary, it did feel a bit harsh, basically having to say, "That's enough, Arlyn! No more goodbyes to your dying Mimi. Get going," but it gave Jude and me a good laugh afterwards.

We watched as they finally walked away with Dad. The emotion of it, their rawness, was palpable. Their beautiful little hearts were breaking. Jude and I again chuckled at the way it had worked out — Papa and his beyond distraught granddaughters. This man, their grandfather, hadn't played the same role as their grandmother clearly had in their young lives at that point, and he didn't express emotion to this extent. He'd confessed on many occasions that he didn't really know what to do with girls, despite having one of his own, and was now the lone adult with them as they processed this experience. He was helping Sam and me, but was in a pivotal role of helping them in their greatest hour of need. It was quite brilliant! Mum would have loved the irony of it!

"Step up, and into yourself, Ralph!" she would have
said.

"You can do this. They need you; I need you to do this
for them. Take care of them. Don't be frightened of them.
You've said you're sorry; that was very important, but so is
this. I am handing them over to you. I expect a lot from you.
They deserve a lot from you. If you're open to it, you will get
so much back. You can do it! Don't let me down on this one."

So then, there were four.

"The gang".

During

Chapter 4 – Waiting

As dusk turned to night, we were informed that we were moving to our own room. I hadn't realised that there were actual rooms, I had just assumed we would stay sharing with Bruce, with only a curtain to pull for people to die behind. Being in no way up to that module, I hadn't even considered how difficult for all involved that would be, in part also because the length of time dying can take was still such an abstract idea to me. My focus was so narrowed to dealing with the reality that Mum was dying, and that it could be at any minute, so I was shocked when they said we were being moved to somewhere more private. It felt like we were being upgraded. I suppose someone had died to free it up for us.

The reality is that people would have very likely died in that shared space while they waited for a room, and if Mum had, in the quiet, "slip away movie style" way I assumed it would happen, the room would have been insignificant to me. As we walked out, I was surprised to realise it was early evening. We had been up very early that morning, but despite that, the day had gone quickly, and somehow Mum was still alive, and we weren't on our way back to Sam's. The nurses wheeled Mum out and said they would make her a bit more comfortable, encouraging us to make ourselves a cuppa and have a break, reassuring us that everything was under control while we waited. I can't remember what Mum was wearing; it must have been in part at least what Sam had found her in because they asked for some fresh clothes and if it would be okay with us if they cut what she had on, so as to minimise her distress. We said no problem, secretly laughing afterwards, that as she wasn't going to be wearing those clothes from now on, we were sure she wouldn't mind. It was strange leaving her side and "handing her over" like that. I wanted to say, "Make sure you come and get us before she dies."

Knowing me, I probably did say something along those lines.

I had barely left Mum's side since early that morning, only to where I was still in view of her to make the call to Dad and one brief visit to the TV room to check up on the kids, so I wasn't aware there was a tearoom with a coffee machine, which was very exciting! I made a cappuccino, how fancy! I was loving the idea of being able to make ourselves a real coffee, not only that, but it was free! I figured even though it was getting late, Mum would surely be dying sometime soon, so a coffee was probably a good idea. It was also a bit of a tragic thrill to be making a cappuccino so close to bedtime.

I sat for a while, consciously using the time to reflect, aware that I needed that time alone. I didn't call anyone to let them know what was happening in my life. No one came in, and there wasn't anyone in the hallway, so I was able to just sit drinking my coffee, feeling perhaps oddly peaceful and happy to be in my own company; almost as though I was on a tea break in a work staff room. Break time over, Sam and Jude came in from wherever it was they had been. We noticed there seemed to be a lot of action in the room directly opposite. Nurses were going in and out in a hurry, closing the door behind them so we couldn't see what was happening. We didn't know where they'd taken Mum, anxiously hoping it wasn't in there, but we were easy to find, so assumed it was possibly someone else's "moment" and Mum must be okay, as no one was looking for us, so we waited. It wasn't our "turn" yet.

After about an hour, we were taken to room 12 — the room where the commotion was coming from. As we entered, everything seemed peaceful. The room was dimly lit by a light over Mum's bed. She looked brighter and refreshed, and she smelled cleaner too. Her nightie read

"Sleep Solves Everything". Well, maybe not *everything,* but we enjoyed that little addition, Mum lying there dying, wearing that. We had only had maybe three hours' sleep in the last 24 hours, but we would have found that funny regardless of our delirium.

A lovely nurse introduced herself as Courtney. She was young and very pretty and seemed more mature than youthful looks suggested. We quickly nicknamed her within "our gang" conversations from then on as "Courts". We hit it off instantly with her and again got the feeling that we had landed in the best place anyone could hope to die. These people really knew their stuff!

We set about making ourselves comfortable. There was a blue fake leather reclining armchair on one side of the bed, and a metal chair with brown vinyl padding on the other. Opposite the bed, there was a bench seat that reclined almost flat to form a small cot-sized bed. There was a large bathroom, and a window with blinds drawn. Opposite Mum's bed, there was a long bench and mirror, a bar fridge and some cupboards. I was still wearing the gym gear that Kel and Sam had kindly washed and dried in the few hours I'd spent there, not thinking to ask Dad to bring anything of mine when he was gathering things for the girls. We weren't anticipating an overnight stay, so none of us had anything with us, but we started settling ourselves in as best we could. What a day, eh, and what a night we had ahead. We discussed how, in retrospect, it was probably good that Mum was going to die tonight, instead of with the kids and everyone else around. She wouldn't have wanted to put the girls through that, and besides, she was a private person who was more suited to dying in this quiet room, tonight, with just the three of us by her side.

Jude happily discovered that in the bag we grabbed from Mum's (conveniently unpacked from her stay at Sam and Kel's on Christmas night), there were a few outfits that fit her, so after her shower, she thanked Mum, telling her she might just "borrow" them for good. Again, to Jude's delight, in another stroke of luck, Mum used the same reflux medication she did, and that was in the bag too. So, despite Jude having brought nothing with her, she was all sorted. Good ol' Mum, eh? Helpful right till the end!

Sam and I had showers (worrying the whole time that she might die while doing so) before settling into our positions. We made a plan that during the short wait, two of us should get some sleep, with someone on "watch duty" for when it was "time". Sam was insistent that someone had to always have a hold of Mum's hand, but after Jude and I negotiated, we eventually agreed that a hand needed to be at least somewhere on her. It was an unspoken understanding that she wouldn't be left alone, but at that time of the night and how tired we were, that wasn't likely to be an issue anyway.

Despite Sam volunteering, Jude insisted she would do the first shift and would alert us immediately if anything looked to be on the cards. "Settled" into our uncomfortable positions, despite my coffee and the sound of Mum's loud snoring echoing throughout the room (if only she had her CPAP machine!) I knew I was done for the day. Falling asleep would be easy; exhaustion was coming to my rescue. I had nothing left, even with the awareness that again, I might wake up to find Mum had died, or, in the best-case scenario, was dying, thumping through my body.

But adrenaline, Mum's snoring, and the uncomfortable cot (which I would come to realise comparatively was actually luxurious) were no match for how fatigued I was. Sam, Mum, and Jude were all perched up together in what became known as "CPAP ally", as all three of them snore and use CPAPs. We joked about how none of us would get any sleep with the snoring choir that would be going on, before I quickly drifted off. Obviously, nothing was going to keep me awake that night. Well, I guess one thing would have.

After about four hours sleep, I awoke feeling like a million bucks, give or take a few thousand. Although clearly nil by mouth, Mum's breakfast was delivered, making me realise that I had not eaten anything the day before, despite the snacks and lunch on offer, aside from coffee and toast at Sam's, and my fancy cappuccino, of course. I hadn't even been drinking water. It was as though the mental load was my only focus and ability to manage, and my physical body was irrelevant and therefore had completely shut itself off. It was only the arrival and the thrill of hospital food, which I have strangely always loved (although in this instance, it was just a disappointing apple and cereal box), that alerted me to realise that. So I had a little pick at it, seeing as how the official guest had lost her appetite.

We had been left to our own devices almost entirely the day before, but day two, a new day, with new "modules", started with a lot more medical information and intervention than what Mum had had (in our time with her, at least) to that point.

First up, we met a beautiful young doctor who explained things very clearly, giving me a much better understanding of what had happened and might happen. She outlined a loose plan and validated the important role we had in Mum's care. She seemed genuinely upset by what Mum had gone through and our situation. When she left, I shared my social work perspective, concerned that she seemed doomed for emotional burnout given the level of empathy she seemed to have. That aside, again, we were aware of how blessed we were to be surrounded by such warmth.

We were so grateful on Mum's behalf too. So often she had encountered people along her life's journey that had no awareness, let alone consideration of her sensitive soul's need for interactions, big or small, to be guided by kindness. She often said she felt invisible, or visible for reasons she didn't see as true or important. I guess even though I knew she felt that way, I didn't always use kindness as my main reference point with her. My own selfish needs and trivial wants so often got in the way. I felt a deep relief that she was being cared for with such respect and compassion, and she wouldn't have to put up with anything other than that ever again.

Courts and her off-sider popped in and out throughout the morning, and amongst the information and possibilities presented to us, it was decided that Mum should be kitted out with a "Niki pump" (also called a "driver") to help manage pain. Thankfully, Sam and I work very well as a team, and agreed that this pre-emptive measure was a good one; however, we didn't feel that Mum was *in* pain. We also knew that aside from having bad reactions to a lot of medications, morphine specifically, Mum was also someone who wouldn't want to miss out on the experience. Rather than be too heavily sedated, she would want to be coherent enough to process dying, even if that meant she wasn't 100% comfortable at all times.

Due to the supportive environment, we felt we could control things to ensure that she wasn't suffering, but could still go through her own "modules" without a heavy interference from medication, for the time being at least. We could feel her processing her life and also her death. We didn't want to take that away from her, but of course, we didn't want her to be in pain. It was a very fine line, a guessing game, but one that we used our intuition, our knowing our mum, to play. We asked to hold back on the level of medication provided until we could feel more certain that she needed it. Agreeing with our reasoning and assessment and honouring our role, the nurses gave Mum a mild dose of an alternative pain medication and a light sedative. Thankfully, she seemed to tolerate both and was still able to communicate with us in a way that worked well whenever she was awake.

I have allowed more doubt about this decision, among others, to enter my mind since then. The luxury of time in retrospect makes you assess things differently, but overall, I still think we got this right. I think she was happy that we didn't rush in to try to solve the "problem" of dying for her, by opting for medication too quickly. Our primary aim, as it had been all along, was to make sure Mum wasn't frightened or alone, and of course that she wasn't suffering. Having said that, we'd shifted to a new understanding of how important it was for the four of us that she remain as conscious, aware, and therefore "with" us for as long as she possibly could, rather than just breathing.

We discussed what we hoped for our own time when it came, and despite Jude being clear that she just wanted to be "knocked out", to essentially be rendered completely comatose by drugs, we agreed that Mum probably wouldn't want that approach. Although she seemed increasingly unconscious outwardly, we knew she was cognisant, and that unnecessarily medicating her would likely rob her of the clarity she clearly had. Rather than relieving her pain, it might make her feel sick, as many medications over the years had had that effect. We were also concerned that medication might make her get stuck in a place in her mind that she didn't want to be while she was trying to die, and it might reduce her already limited ability to communicate with us. It didn't appear as though she was in pain, so we worked from a strengths-based perspective and were supported with the perfect balance of privacy and assistance from the caring team. They had the medical knowledge, but our knowledge and ideas were also respected. By lunchtime, a lot of information had been provided, new interventions were in place, and they pretty much left us to it once again.

Since the very beginning, from the time Sam had found Mum, Jude had taken on the role of conduit between us and the outside world. She continued to make and receive many calls that day, updating the sisters in Perth and northern New South Wales that Mum was still hanging on, and fielding requests from family living more locally to visit. By this stage, we felt we'd moved to another module, and it was better for Mum that we preserve the private and quiet little haven for her, and for us, to relax into.

Initially, these requests seemed almost bizarre. How on earth could anyone else penetrate this bubble? We had formed such a tight connection, totally consumed with what was happening inside our "realm". We had to remind ourselves that people living in the "outside world" would be experiencing Mum's impending death differently. People do come and visit people while they are dying, after all. Regardless, it didn't feel right, and we felt confident in our decision to apologise but decline because we knew that's what Mum would want. The four of us had already established "the gang", and for the time being, we weren't taking on new members.

So much had changed since the day before, and as her condition seemed to be deteriorating, we didn't want to go back to waiting for anyone other than her, rushing or second-guessing things, or even concerning ourselves in any way with the world as it existed outside of that room.

However, this plan was short-lived. As the morning rolled along, we were made aware that Brisbane was on the brink of a COVID-related lockdown starting at 6 p.m. that day, the first one of its kind. This news, of course, stepped us back into action mode, with plans for Ev to come back to get the girls. It was arranged that Kel would bring them back to the hospital to not only shave a bit of time off Ev's journey so he could work a few more hours, but also to bring Sam some clothes and say another goodbye to Mum before the three days of lockdown started.

Considering Mum hadn't actually died "as planned" last night, Kel figured she may as well take the opportunity. We decided it was best that Orla and Arlyn didn't see Mum again, which they agreed with. Besides, after the emotion of the day before, they were very content being spoiled by Aunty Judi buying them Maccas and being allowed to play on the computer, both of which they considered exciting treats. They spent a lovely few hours in the tearoom by themselves, keeping out of everyone's way, but close enough for us to keep an occasional eye on them as they pigged out on nuggets and lemonade and played quietly on Orla's laptop. Mum would've been happy that they were relaxed, so well behaved and self-sufficient as they supported each other in such an innocent way.

Sam asked Kel to drop into the bottle-o on her way to get him some Guinness, concerned that a presumed mad rush on booze would mean he'd be left high and dry. He wanted to have something to toast Mum with when he got home, a nod to our Irish heritage, but mainly because he just really likes Guinness and figured that he'd be needing a drink then! Kel misunderstood what he'd asked, putting a four-pack in the fridge when she arrived with his bag. An hour or so later, Ev arrived with my stuff and said another goodbye to Mum before leaving with the girls to fight it out on the highway with the masses of people fleeing to get north of Morayfield in an attempt to escape the impending lockdown that was only in force in the southern region of South East Queensland.

When I said goodbye, it didn't cross my mind when I would see them next. Not because of the lockdown, or a timeframe around Mum dying, I was just so inwardly consumed by being in "the bubble" that normal thought processes like that were beyond me. My focus was narrowed to Mum in a way it had never been before. I had never spent more than a day or two away from my girls, yet I didn't give a thought to being away from them for three days, or beyond that timeframe if the lockdown was to be extended, regardless of what Mum's "plans" were. I had separated myself from "reality" without really knowing it. Looking back, I was already a very different person from the one who existed only 48 hours ago. A drastic change in such a short time and the beginnings of the new me that I'm very grateful I had the chance to become, despite everything.

With everyone gone and only infrequent check-ins from the staff, Sam and I settled back in while Jude was outside attending to her job of being our correspondent. Holding her hands, we sat either side of Mum while she slept, our heads resting on the bed against her body. We weren't doing much talking; it was just quiet time together, hanging out between the two worlds, waiting, without any pressure. This was our family: Mum, Sam, and me. A small family, but with a lot going on within it. The three of us had been through a lot. We weren't perfect; we weren't always our best versions of ourselves with each other, but we were always deeply connected. We knew the core of each other; after all, we had each other, in each other. We fought, we laughed, we supported each other, we irritated the shit out of each other. Lying there together, we were loving each other more than we ever had before. The love was so strong you could feel it on your skin. Is that a shame? Maybe. Maybe we should have been able to feel that depth of love other times, or always, without just relying on knowing it was there. When we could have embraced it into our actual lives, used it in a way that was more meaningful while we were all "living" together, rather than at this time of death.

I don't know, though. Maybe that kind of love, the intensity of that feeling, can only be felt in instances like that. The overpowering emotion you have when you see your child for the first time or, conversely, sit with someone you love as they die. Maybe that's how it works. A both crippling and soaring version of love that is specifically only available for those two miraculous experiences.

The three of us soaked up that quiet time alone, calm and relaxed, just as Mum liked it, resting peacefully with the sound of her snoring. Then she started making some different noises. We hadn't really seen or heard Mum make any movements or noises indicating discomfort, aside from the "incident" with the priest. Her only noise was an occasional grunt and the very loud snoring that she had been doing on and off all day since the night before (she didn't have her CPAP, so we were letting her off the hook with that). Initially, when they needed to move Mum from one position to another, we would leave the room. She needed to endure that procedure, despite it being quite strenuous on her limp and weakened body, in order to remain comfortable for longer periods, but the staff felt it would be unnecessarily stressful for us to witness. As we became "seasoned campaigners", we would stay in the room with the curtains drawn. She didn't sound too bothered, but this noise was new and it seemed to be changing, if not also intensifying.

That morning, we had a discussion with the staff about the death rattles. Sam and I, as with most of our death knowledge, knew about this from the movies. As a nurse, Jude was very familiar, but she'd also sat by her own (actual) mother's bedside while she was dying. We knew that it was an indicator that the body was breaking down, preparing to let go of life. Sam and I lifted our heads to look at each other as if to say,

"Did you hear that"?

"Is that a death rattle"?

"Is it happening"?

As the sound built, we realised that *was* what was happening. The time had come. Mum was dying.

Once we'd taken a moment or two to let this realisation land, Sam hurried off to get Jude and tell the nurses. The time had come. Sam and Jude were back within a few minutes, followed by a nurse who checked Mum and assured us that she wasn't in pain before leaving to give us privacy.

The three of us sat around Mum, deeply focusing on our love and intentions for her. The sound was loud and was becoming constant. We sat there for probably less than 10 minutes, waiting, shocked that this was actually happening. We'd been waiting, not really willing (yet) but waiting, expecting, and now, this was how it was going to be. This distressing sound. Even with all the effort we'd made to make sure she was relaxed and secure, she would be going out sounding like she was drowning, uncomfortable, in pain, possibly even, but this was how it worked. This is how people die. This is how Mum would die: drowning in fluid at the back of her throat. I wished she could cough. I wished she could sit up, spit, and relieve herself of the discomfort or irritation of this horrible feeling, then lie back down and die quietly and peacefully. But the noise kept on. She wasn't dying. Well, she was very clearly still breathing is maybe a better way to put it, and in more ways than one, that was the problem.

We asked Jude to get the nurse back. Mum clearly needed help. Someone needed to do something! It seemed like she was trying, but struggling to die. It was as though she couldn't do it. Although she knew what she knew, Jude understood our panic and shared our distress, so she went to find someone. In a strange and sort of funny way, I remember thinking, *Hurry up! She needs help! If this keeps going on for too long, she could die!* then realising how confusing that thought was. I was *so* anxious. I couldn't stand seeing her like that. I couldn't bear the idea of that even happening to her, let alone witnessing it. When someone sounds like that, they die, that's why it's called the death rattle, isn't it? The last thing that happens before you die. Yet, she was still breathing, without really being able to do either, breathe or die.

Something was going wrong. Something had to be done. In hindsight, we were only up to Module 1.31 — "Signs of dying don't mean that death is imminent". We didn't know, Sam and I at least didn't, that yes, this was a sign, but our rookie experience made us assume this process would be relatively quick, five minutes maybe, max. The nurse came in and informed us (much to our horror) that this sound doesn't necessarily mean you will die straight away, even though it does in the movies. Who would have thought, eh? No timeframe could be given with any certainty. From this moment forward, there were many times when changes in her breathing made us think it was "game on". Several times we would stop, look at each other, brace ourselves, only to find that it was just another of her "pranks". As a result, we bestowed her with her own nickname, "The Queen of False Alarms". After all, the leading lady needed a title in this epic drama.

So, she just continued with the process she needed to go through. She wasn't at her destination just yet. This was "okay", "quite normal", so we were told! So very quickly we went from feelings of heartache, distraught, anxiety, and tension as we braced for her death, to a scene where Mum's positioning was changed and she was provided with more medication, both of which we were told would help, but not cure, the rattling (there was only one remedy for that). We remained by her side, while she just kept on crackling, gurgling. Somehow, it became part of our day. The soundtrack we had never imagined and hadn't requested. We returned to our focus of making sure she wasn't alone or frightened, and strangely, despite this horrible noise that was becoming oddly acceptable, she wasn't in pain. The interventions seemed to be doing the trick of keeping her relaxed despite sounding to the contrary.

As the day kept ticking along, the nurses continued to reposition Mum every few hours. After one of these adjustments, it became clear that Mum was still uncomfortable. It hadn't provided the relief it had on previous occasions. Rather than ask the nurses to shift her again, we decided to see if adjusting the angle of the bed might help, figuring that if we just made it a bit more upright, gravity might help. The rattle seemed to be coming from deeper in the back of her throat, so we thought maybe that was irritating her. We pressed the control pad without success. We couldn't seem to get the bed to do what we wanted, but kept trying, in vain, as, without a word being spoken, a collective thought struck us all at once.

Eyeballing each other, we were considering whether, in fact, we should be trying to solve this problem. Were we helping her, or prolonging the inevitable? After all, this could be the answer to what the four of us were there for. Maybe we should just leave her be so she could "get it done". Trying to contain the evil laughter bubbling up in all of us, we decided we should continue to try to help her, although dismally failing in our attempt to get our "Hospital Bed Licence", as the bed went in every other direction than how we were attempting to drive it.

We took turns, disagreeing and giving advice, despite having no luck when having the controller, and before we knew what we'd done, we had Mum facing feet first at a very steep angle, looking like she might slide downhill, onto the floor. Keep in mind that this was happening within only a few hours of when we'd first heard the horrendous suffering sound of the death rattles, one of the most powerfully gut-wrenching moments in our lives, and the desperation and intense shock we'd experienced believing Mum was *actually about to die*.

Yet there we stood, as the gurgling in its "new normal" way continued; killing ourselves laughing, absolutely losing it in a no sound coming out, almost wetting our pants type of way. She looked like Bernie from the movie *Weekend at Bernie's*. Continuing to "fix it" just kept making it worse, and therefore funnier, as we worried that any moment the nurses would come in and bust us for being silly and for nearly making our dying mother slip out of bed.

Finally, we composed ourselves and managed to make the angle slightly less drastic, as best we could, to not cause alarm, and went to let a nurse know that Mum's new position (the one they had put her in, nothing to do with our reckless driving) didn't seem to be working for her.

Chapter 5 — Rollercoaster

As the afternoon progressed, we continued to settle into both our surroundings and the process. I decided to take a break by having a shower, to pass the time more than anything, opting not to change into the strapless bra or other bizarre items of clothing Ev had packed for me. His choices provided us with yet another chuckle as we imagined what was going through his mind when he packed for me to sit by Mum's bedside in palliative care, "A strapless push-up bra? Yes, she'll be needing one of those."

Freshened up, now with another evening approaching, our bond was deepening, our experience of life and death expanding. A radiant late afternoon summer sun shower started, diverting our attention outside and making us aware that it was Friday afternoon and the perfect time for a drink! We still had the Guinness in the fridge! What a stroke of good luck that Kel had forgotten to take it with her, the luck of the Irish perhaps! It would be rude not to crack one.

Jude was having a break from alcohol at the time and, surprisingly to us all (including her), even stuck to that plan on Christmas Day, despite Kel, Mum, and me knocking back a wide variety of delicious cocktails, but she decided a few sips of black gold couldn't hurt. It was basically medicinal in Ireland anyway, so her "no drinking rule" didn't really apply.

We settled in around Mum as the rain fell, bringing with it it's comforting summer rain smell, and the sun started its trip down towards the horizon. A beautiful time of day made more so by the rain sparkling in the orange afternoon sun. A beautiful time of the day to die. We discussed that for many reasons, we all hoped this would be the time it happened for us when our time came and considering Mum was not much of a morning person, she would likely agree, so we settled ourselves in for her last sunset.

The Guinness cracked, and the sun was fading through the clouds, so we realised we needed some tunes. We hadn't played any music since Mum's instruction not to when we were on the ward, but she was sleeping, and we were sure she would agree that music was now warranted. It was Friday drinks after all. Even if she didn't want it on, what was she going to do about it, eh?

Music playing, we sipped on our drinks and kind of fell into having a lovely little send-off party. We played everything from Frank Sinatra's *My Way*, which we found hilarious because it really isn't a song befitting of Mum at all, all the way through to country tunes she loved and many other genres in between. As is our way, every song had meaning and was chosen for a purpose. We played Xavier Rudd's *Follow the Sun*, listening with reverence, overcome by the words and vibration it creates. We commented that not only was it now a perfect time, but also the perfect song to die to, at that time of day. We made a platter from the untouched food Jude was bringing in from her numerous reconnaissance missions, we sang and reminisced, we debriefed on the events of the last few days, and we delighted in each other's company, Mum's included, of course.

The strong bond of family was very powerful on that pretty afternoon. We knew each other so deeply, as though we could feel our bloodline running through the four of us. We shared a can (okay, maybe it was two) of Guinness and were flying high. Floating again, but this time buoyant because of our connection, and therefore our strength was at a peak.

We shared memories and stories, some about crazy things that had nothing to do with anything in particular, like broken fridge seals and weird topics like that, causing long bouts of hysterical laughter so hard that it's almost silent and you can barely breathe as you wipe tears from your eyes. We also cried tears of sadness. We were on the verge of losing the person who was responsible for shaping the connection we shared. Surrounding Mum, we cried, we sang, we hugged. This party in her honour was one of the best I've ever been to. We even gave her a few little "sips" of Guinness, dabbing it on her smiling bottom lip for her to suck off. Why should she miss out?

We discussed who might come to greet her when she got to where she was going, excited for her; it was also a thoroughly fun guessing game to play. We initially assumed it would be Uncle Michael, Jude and Mum's brother. We imagined him already quietly and patiently waiting in his gentle way, and that he would reach out his hand and smile his big smile at her when it was time. Or would she hear "the whistle" and follow it to whoever was whistling? Of course! That would be it, the way it would happen! That meant it would probably be Dadda, our grandfather, Jude and Mum's father. He would whistle the family whistle — the McCabe Whistle, the long version that signals you're not in trouble or being summoned to hurry. The style that's to get your attention, whistled loud and slow so you can follow its tune in a crowd to its source. He would finally appear in the distance once mum was sure she was hearing it clearly, walk towards her, still whistling, then he would grab her around the shoulders and squeeze her in close to him in one of his almost too-tight hugs, and safely lead her to where she needed to go.

Who else would be there, we wondered? All the people she had "unearthed" and brought to life through the long hours she spent studying our family history would certainly be there! Annie Hart, as well as her four grandparents, no doubt. She would get to meet her maternal grandmother Ena and connect as three generations for the first time! What a great reunion and celebration it would be! A kick arse party was already getting underway no doubt in anticipation of her arrival, while we were having one to send her there. Without planning it, we were sending her off perfectly. A celebration with everything she could hope for. Beautiful weather as the sun was setting, music, laughter, tears, connection, and even an Irish twist. A perfect way to die.

I was so grateful and happy that Mum seemed comfortable, despite her laboured breathing, and was able to *be* at the party, that she wasn't so sedated that she missed out. We could feel her floating with us. She was quite likely floating higher than all of us, watching us from her bird's-eye view when she felt like it and re-joining us for moments like her little Guinness smile. We could feel her happiness and were feeding off it, perhaps. In my life before the stroke, as well as my life within those few days, it is one of my favourite memories. The joy within that room was stronger than any medication, despair, or exhaustion. It was a celebration of her and of our family, and celebrate we did.

With the sun set, the rain continuing, and the drinks drunk, we found ourselves realising that the "perfect time to die" had been and gone. Mum was still with us, still rattling, still snoring, still hanging on. How could it be?

Only two weeks ago, Mum was enjoying one of the best Christmases our family had ever had, with none of this anywhere near the horizon as far as we all knew. But she did have a myriad of long-standing health issues. Heart problems, blood pressure problems, mobility problems, digestive problems, gynaecological problems, breathing problems, and mental health problems. We had been told three days ago that she had suffered a "massive stroke", *massive*, and to top that off, also a heart attack. For days, she had lain alone on her kitchen floor, in the heat, with no food or drink. She had now been in the hospital for two days, with nothing but a drip on arrival to sustain her, yet she was still here. We could see, but more so hear, her body losing its way, but somehow it was not giving up. The party was over, but she wasn't ready to leave. Another moonrise was underway, and the four of us were still together. So, onto the next module we all went.

As the activity of the day slowed down, we prepared for another night in our new "home". The nurses continued to move Mum and provide her with medication to remain as comfortable as we could only guess she was. We were getting to know everyone better, laughing with them that yes, we were still here, as their shift rolled around again. We met a very attentive and compassionate nurse named

Kate, whom we related to as if she were family. She would go on to become an invaluable resource of both comfort and support for our ideas on how things should progress with Mum's care.

It was becoming easier for us to recognise that the medication was doing what we hoped, and as we'd been advised would happen, every four hours or so, we were able to identify ourselves to ask the nurses to "top her up" and could see it was necessary that they increase her dosage. Going into the second night, she was less frequently awake and no longer communicating in any way. Despite this, we knew she was busy processing. The intensity of her concentration had shifted inwardly, and she was no longer concerned with her external physical world.

She had a different job now. A new focus that required stepping across from our bubble into her own bubble to provide her with the quiet and the cushioning from ours that she needed, whilst still being able to see through and gently bump up against us from time to time. While we continued through our modules, we figured she was perhaps starting some postgraduate courses.

As was her style in living, she needed to take time, reflect, and be still in order to die. To process things so they made sense, enabling her to proceed with confidence. Unlike my responses then, I have clarity about this now. I don't reflect on it being drawn out at all. I know now that if you are blessed enough to be given the opportunity of time, the many modules associated with dying can't be rushed.

Although 67 years is young to die, 67 years of life, of living *her* life, would of course require time to contemplate, untangle, and absorb all the layers. But while she was doing so, I was tired. I was in uncharted waters. I was fearful on some levels, impatient on others, and was overwhelmed by shock, with only a very simplistic level of understanding that any of that was happening. I could feel her teaching and helping me, but to a lesser extent than I am able to recognise now. The three of us understood that she wasn't just lying there doing nothing, but I wanted the process to be quicker because I thought that meant easier. Subconsciously, I was struggling with my own version of untangling the layers, consciously focusing on "the moment" finally arriving and feeling like I *needed* it to be over soon, rather than releasing into the flow.

I read something after Mum died, written by someone my age who had also been with her mother as she died. Her mother had suffered from a long illness. I don't know if that makes a difference, but she sat by her bedside pleading with her not to die, and it struck me that not once while I sat with Mum did I do that. In fact, strangely, I was doing the opposite. Why had I not once thought *Live, live*?

I was concentrating on her death so strongly, not in any way because I wanted her dead, but I had just "accepted" that was her fate. I'm sure that woman knew there was no way her mum could just sit up and keep living for her, but her immense love didn't see reason. Whereas, despite the depth of emotions I was experiencing, my love kept my logic intact, and increasingly by this stage, with no thought, absolutely zero contemplation even of how life would be without her, I was very focused on the facts. I have always been, by nature, an impatient person, and there I was, not realising the full extent that this was an opportunity to have more time with her, talk through things, or tell her every hour of those days, multiple times each hour if I wanted to, how loved she was. From time to time, I found myself feeling desperate for her to go. The depth of these uncharted waters was so deep, and trying to keep my head above the water was so utterly exhausting.

I know this should probably make me feel heavy with guilt. It doesn't. I know how much I loved my mum and how much I wish she was still alive, but I guess it demonstrates how people respond so differently to the same thing life throws out. Fatigue was certainly playing a big role in everything by now. The energy of that room was being dominated by tiredness, love, and humour, quite a wonderful mix for such an occasion.

Despite being in a situation that was making us more connected than we had ever been, all four of us were experiencing it differently and therefore responding from inside our own comprehension. The bubbles within the bubble. My bubble felt like a very complex, at times suffocating and draining place to be. I didn't know how long I could keep floating around like that. Getting so used to seeing my mum lying there, dying, let alone hearing it happening.

Although I hadn't looked at a clock for days, I was aware it was getting late, so I had another shower as a means of taking a break before we settled ourselves in for the night. Sam had the recliner, Jude the cot, and I was in the chair. We continued chatting and laughing and then did that thing you do when you sleep over with your friends. "Good nights", are said, the conversation stops, then out of nowhere, someone pipes up with one more topic, one more joke. Despite the circumstances, it was nice, even sort of fun, to be together like that.

Eventually, the frequency of these little bursts waned, and it was just the sound of Mum, snoring and struggling to breathe, rattling. Regardless, I eventually drifted off to sleep. I don't think I'd been asleep long when I was woken by a sound I quickly recognised as being different. It was like a muffled gasp. As my eyes adjusted, I saw Jude standing over Mum. It was dark, but small slivers of light were coming in under the door from the hallway, and from the courtyard that I had yet to venture into, in small part due to the weather, but mainly because my "institutionalised" brain had not considered doing so. From what I could make out, Jude seemed relatively calm, but once I shook myself awake more, I realised something was wrong. Mum was gagging.

As I walked towards them, I could see that Mum's nose seemed to be bleeding. She was also sort of foaming around her mouth and appeared aware and distressed. It was horrifying, but more so, unbearable, seeing her suffering in such a bizarre way. Jude was talking to her quietly and kindly, while wiping her face, but the thick black discharge kept leaking from her nose. It looked like leeches crawling out of her. It looked utterly mental. Crazy. Not real. Mum was semi-conscious and was bothered by it, but seemed sedated enough that had she not been, she would have been reacting far worse. I was absolutely freaked out, so intensely confronted by what I was seeing that I couldn't process it. I felt like everything was in slow motion. I was stunned, probably in actual shock, wondering if I was dreaming because it felt like a nightmare.

This stuff was coming out of Mum's nose and slowly sliding down the side of her mouth. Jude was composed, but she must have buzzed for help because some nurses brushed past me as I stood dumbfounded, mind blown, trying to get my brain and eyes to connect so that I could work out what to do or how to feel. Jude would have started trying to explain things, I am sure, and I would have asked if Mum was okay, despite it being evident to anyone looking at what I was looking at, that the answer was "No." But probably my main question would have been:

"Is this it?"

Jude and the nurses started explaining that this was "normal". Normal! Yeah, right! That could not be true! Apparently, there is more than just the death rattles, as if they aren't enough. As Jude was talking me through it, she told me my grandmother had also gone through this when she died. What the hell was this all about? This weird secret that gets sprung on you while you're watching your mum die, just trying to contend with "the basics" of that! How on earth had I been alive for almost 44 years, and never, ever, once in my whole life, heard of this "normal" process? This "other" part of dying?!

I could hear myself screaming *What the fuck, what the fuck!* inside my head. After witnessing and then learning to deal with this "thing", there is now a part of me that understands the reason behind it being "secret dying business". People don't talk about death much as it is, let alone this beyond bizarre, disgusting, poltergeist-like, yet also, in my opinion formed since, sacred part of it.

Despite the commotion of what was happening to Mum, Jude and I talking, and two nurses arriving, Sam remained fast asleep on the recliner, right in the thick of the action, until he was abruptly awoken by a third nurse bumping into his leg as she rushed in. He sat upright, attempting to shake himself awake, while Jude began to explain things to him, as I listened on, still in a state of panicked numbness. You can imagine his confusion and shock. He was clearly out cold from having very little sleep, only to be woken and immediately told of this "development" as it was happening right at eye level in front of him. Poor Samby. I was so sad that my big little brother had to see his mum like that.

The Secretions.

That's what the nurses told us it was called. I haven't made that up.

Secretions. Such an unfortunately perfect description of what it is. Shocking. Disturbing. Horrifying. Unbelievable. The rattle had now changed to more of a gurgle, which was the sound that had woken me. The fact that this can happen, and what it looks like, is one thing. It could even be thought of as interesting; I guess it is, but the main part I struggled with was the shock. I still can't understand how I had no knowledge of its existence, not even via the trusty old movies. If I had, I would have assumed it was fictional anyway. I certainly had never had a discussion with anyone recounting their experience of it, so this newfound knowledge was just as bizarre to me as the process itself.

I used to think about it a lot in the weeks after Mum's death, but it hasn't been something I've thought of now for many months. Since then, I have watched many documentaries and read many books on death, yet I still have not come across this topic discussed, making it feel as though it is supposed to remain a mystery until you die or be with someone while they do. I find it strange that in this world of so much information sharing, it's not more common knowledge. Perhaps because the death rattles are harrowing enough, it's been "decided" to let that be known, but stop there.

Obviously, it was a horrible experience made harder by being so unprepared, but in just a short time after Mum died, I started conceptualising it as less of a secret and more like a private or even remarkable experience to be a part of. Within this broader story, it was such a pivotal moment for me, so after considering whether I should keep "the secret", I felt I must include what could be considered confidential, "inside knowledge". Whether that is for good or for bad, I am not sure, but I guess the cat is out of the bag now to anyone reading this who, like me, has never heard of it!

Mum had obviously suffered extreme dehydration before she was found by Sam. Tests she underwent that night discovered that she was experiencing multiple organ failure, in particular, her kidneys, which was why she was deemed palliative so quickly. Rehabilitation from the viewpoint of her stroke was not considered; she was already well into organ failure mode. I know this because I have since discussed it with Jude. It only occurred to me a few months *after* she died that I didn't really know why she had been assessed as palliative; it just made sense after what she had endured. I'd been busy with other thoughts, it seems. Quite likely this would have been explained, and perhaps I did take it in, but then became overloaded.

In retrospect, it seems like I just accepted the news that she was going to die so readily. I didn't ask for a second opinion; I was told she was palliative and went with it. A strange reaction, perhaps?

Anyway, the drip that she was initially given in the emergency department had sustained her until this time. I had asked several times on the first day if she should be given another drip, worried that the plan was essentially to starve her to death to get it over with, but was told that her body was in a state of limbo and exerting so little energy that she didn't require food or water. That seemed impossible, which is why I asked a few times before eventually accepting it. Jude has since explained, as she probably did then, that if she were given another drip, her organs would not be able to process it, so it would have done her more harm than good.

It was being explained to Sam and me, as we watched this gruesome scene, that the secretions were being brought about by the drip. Basically, her organs couldn't process that liquid. That was also the reason Mum seemed so puffy, so soft and bloated and her rattle was so wet and deep. Her organs seemed to be disintegrating, "melting", and escaping out of her mouth and nose. A thick black and dark red sludge oozing out of her as she choked and struggled to breathe, but somehow astonishingly, still did. The other strange part of it, as if we needed more, was that she didn't seem overly distressed, even though she looked as though she was possessed, like she was in a horror movie. It even had a weird smell that really wasn't helping things. It was unreal, an out-of-body-cannot-comprehend-it thing to witness. Something you wouldn't want anyone to go through, let alone one of the people you care for most in the world.

I suppose it's like the first time you watch the body birth someone, how confronting and mind-blowing that can be. Not in every scenario, I acknowledge, but hopefully with birth, you are anticipating something positive, so comprehending the craziness is made a little easier because of that. Watching the body do something so drastic, confusing, and almost violent, without any hope of joy when it's over, is something that changes you. You'll never forget something like that.

The nurses explained they could drain the fluid to provide Mum some relief, but more so to help us, as apparently it is the people watching their loved one endure this madness who suffer more. Who really knows that to be true, though? No one is coming back from that to tell the tale. They said they would do this at regular intervals because once drained, the secretions would continue to build up, explaining that this draining process would be unpleasant for Mum but that in their experience (of never having had that crap coming out of them) it would be worth it, because it would ease the irritation and make her more comfortable. This new intervention could be incorporated into what they were already doing for her. Although we had built up an immunity to the discomfort Mum had to go through to be helped, they suggested it would be best if we left the room. It would be too confronting for loved ones to see or hear it being done (*let alone loved ones who have only just learnt about this insane, gruesome, apparently normal part of death 10 minutes ago*, was what I thought). Trusting their guidance and with Jude's reassurance, we left and let them do their thing.

Mum was so much better when we went back in, and we all went back to our stations. What the hell? When was this going to be over? With Mum clean and back to "normal", exhaustion grabbed me by the hand and yanked me back to sleep until I was once again shaken from its depths. Nurses were rushing in, and Jude was again standing beside Mum, who sounded like she was completely drowning, unable to swallow or cough up the fluid gurgling at the back of her throat. She seemed more aware and distressed by it than she had originally, and there seemed to be more of a heightened sense of urgency in the room. I guessed it was around midnight, perhaps slightly later, only two or three hours since the last episode. What they did to help Mum earlier obviously needed to be done again. I got up and stood watching Mum with everyone around her, again gut-punched by what I was seeing.

These fucking sick secretions, upsetting her, hurting her, possessing her, taking away her peace and her ability to die with dignity — I could not stand it. I could not do this anymore. I couldn't cope with this drawn-out, increasingly worse, still-not-over way of existing. Every time I woke up from the heavy black nothingness of my sleep to find her still struggling, it felt like an electric shock, instantly frying my brain and shattering my heart into pieces. I needed it to finally be over. I couldn't stay on this scary ride anymore. Mum could not do this anymore. I couldn't cope with Sam and Jude having to do this anymore. I asked Courts how long this was likely to go on for. How much longer did we all have to deal with this? Her response sent me into a derailment.

"It could be soon, or it could be days," she said.

"I've seen people go through this for days."

FOR DAYS.

Upon hearing this, I ran into the bathroom, fell to my knees, hunched into a ball and screamed into my stomach. I screamed as hard as I fucking could, but my choking and crying prevented me from releasing my fury as intensely as I was feeling it. I was so angry at the universe for taking the magic away from Mum, robbing her of her peace and forcing this fucked up bullshit of a way to die on her. Drowned to death by her own thick, black, smelly, mucous-filled, disgusting, rotting organs. What the fuck! Why in the fuck was this happening like this?! My beautiful, gentle Mum. My kind, soft, loving, and fascinating Mum, having to go through this, and the universe, which she had always done right by, spitting in her face like this. Spitting its revolting, stinking black snot right in her face. I wanted to punch the universe. I was so insulted by it. I wanted to strangle something. I could not and would not accept that this was part of my mum's story. I remember *screaming* repeatedly,

"Don't take the magic away, don't take the magic away."

She deserved so much more than this. We had come so far on this journey together, of life together even before these past few days, and had done everything in our power since finding her to protect her and ensure that she was sent off with joy and love, and now this was happening! This completely unforeseen part of the story just couldn't be real.

I was shattered. I was at the lowest point I had ever been in my life. I was exhausted, but I was not having it. Inside my head, I yelled at the universe to fucking get its shit together and stop doing this to one of its purest daughters. I yelled at my grandparents and my uncle to make it stop! *Why are you letting this happen?! You are supposed to be helping her, coming for her! Not letting her be drowned by this evil devil sap! Somebody whistle for her, for fuck's sake!* Incoherently screaming, and moaning, I felt like I was insane. I was enraged. I had lost every ounce of self-control. I was a wild animal caught in a trap. Jude and one of the nurses came in to try to help me, to comfort me, but also quite possibly to try to quieten and calm me down. Looking back, what a horrible thing for anyone else lying there in the other rooms to have heard.

I felt very guilty, once time had passed, and I had that realisation. I was wailing, swearing, pleading. The walls and door would not have completely blocked the intensity of the sounds of my pain from other patients at Mum's end of the building.

Among all the other moments that we have pulled apart to understand or just reminisce about, Sam, Jude, and I have discussed that from the beginning to the end of us being there, apart from staff, we saw so few people. Bruce had a few visitors that first day, and during daytime hours, we would see the odd person, but for the most part, it seemed to be just us. We seemed to have the run of the place whenever we'd get some fresh air in the courtyards or make a cuppa in the tearoom. At night, we didn't cross paths with anyone. Not to say there wasn't anyone there, but if so, we didn't see them. The nurses told us that they support many people who would otherwise die alone, in most cases, not because they are not loved, but a vigil like we were keeping is not something that all people are able, or want to do. So, lying there in whatever state of what we know as consciousness they were in, waiting for death perhaps alone in the dark that night, there may have been people hearing me, losing my mind. Screaming out my pain. I feel horrible when I consider that I may have caused others distress. I know Mum could hear me. Connected to me as she was, she certainly knew what I was dealing with, regardless of her conscious state, but I know I didn't scare her. She would've just been focused on me, wanting to comfort me. I think by that stage she might have been beyond seeing things from a basic, human, approach. She probably knew it was a necessary part of my process. She could sit with pain, mine or her own. I think she was maybe even hovering around in there watching me in the harsh fluorescent lights of that bathroom, feeling proud of me for being so strong *and* so vulnerable.

I eventually recovered enough to open my eyes, get up, and let my rage lift a little. I had really, really lost it. I washed my face, got a cup of tea, and went back in to be with Mum. After another drain, she was much better. I sat next to her on the window side. Jude was in the recliner. She, of the three of us, had had the least amount of sleep as she was so busy being so supportive of Sam and me, taking care of Mum's children, in her role as our "aunt". She was going through her own grief, as a sister, being "the nurse", answering our questions, reliving the death of her own mother, reporting back and forth to everyone in the outside world, all the while dealing with her own health issues, one of which was insomnia. Sam was sleeping, his big body lying contorted on the cot-sized bed. He looked so pale, and beyond wiped out. It was somewhere between 3 and 4 a.m. Witching hour.

Sam and Jude fell asleep. I held Mum's hand, talking to her in my head because I knew by then that was a perfectly valid way of communicating, and I didn't want to disturb Sam and Jude. Sleep was such a precious necessity. I felt the beginnings of a new day coming forth. Another day for Mum to fight. Was she fighting? Or was she being robbed of any control? I sat watching Jude and Sam sleep, looking at Mum, dying. I watched her dying for a while and cried softly. I was so tired. I started talking to my nanna, having realised that it was probably *she* who would be coming to collect Mum! Ah, of course! That's a mother's job. Taking their child's hand, reassuring them when they're leading them to new places and into new experiences. It would be Nanna! How had we not realised that? But why? Why was she taking so long, letting her suffer like this? She must know Mum had endured enough. I couldn't understand Nanna's lack of empathy or logic. She was a good mum, a great nanna, yet she was allowing this very drawn-out and increasingly tragic experience for us all. She should be making it happen with the magic we were dreaming of for Mum. She had that ability, surely. Why wasn't she using it?

I sat, fighting with my nanna, who I loved so dearly. Never had I ever had a bad word to say to her or of her. But I was pissed off, and I let her know it. I knew our relationship could handle it. I was gripping my rose quartz, pressing it hard into my palm, quietly crying, and confronting Nanna in my head. Pleading with her, with anyone "out there" really, to hurry up and do "the whistle". Let her know it's time. This longest of McCabe goodbyes needed a conclusion. It's really time to go. Whistle her, please, louder if you are, because she can't hear you. Make it the "quick, get your arse here now" version. The "you're in trouble" style. Nanna was forever rushing her. It had always been a deep issue of Mum's. She felt like she'd spent her childhood being told to "Hurry up, Eil!".

So where was she? It was clearly time. Why was Nanna letting her dawdle now, of all times?

My thinking began to shift. I started to wonder if maybe it was me? Maybe I had some kind of power that I wasn't using properly, and *I* could make it happen for Mum.

Holy shit, of course! That was probably the answer! I was holding myself too tight, forcing things, focused on her dying so much. Maybe that was suffocating her, rather than allowing her spirit to be free and release itself from her body. I relaxed back in my chair, feet up on another chair, stretching my arm out on the bed, the rose quartz resting in my open palm.

I breathed, slowly, really slowly, in, and out, using relaxation techniques Mum had taught me when I was an anxious little child. I imagined my spot beneath the tree. The big tree that hung over the crystal-clear creek down the back of some acreage where Mum had once lived near Byron Bay, where we had once seen a platypus. I slowed myself right down. After the fight, all the swearing and anger I had just directed at Nanna, I needed to redirect my approach. If this was it, if I was the key, if I could really make this happen, I needed to breathe and implement the skills Mum had given me, those "hippie things" she instilled in me that made her different from all the other mums when I was a little girl.

I did a "releasing process" for her, imagining a luminous shimmering silver and pink light, beaming out from the quartz, up towards heaven. I visualised Mum ascending into it and becoming part of it. She was immersed, fading into the light and floating away, just like that. I raised the quartz high above my head, directing the light so it knew where to go. Maybe I needed to be that specific? I wondered if I should even wake Jude and Sam if it happened. It would just be so effortless, quiet, and whenever they finally woke from their heavy slumber, they would be rested, Mum would be lying there, finally dead, and I would tell them gently that it was okay. It was over, but it had been so *easy*. Just like she went to sleep, but with all the beauty that we had hoped for.

But still she gurgled. I remained relaxed but realised I was still forcing it. I also realised how delirious I was feeling and how very unlikely it was that I had the power to make my mother's body rise up from the bed into a light in the darkness, made by a crystal I was holding in my hand, while listening to a long, ethereal-sounding McCabe whistle

I could hear coming from another dimension.

So, I just continued to sit and be still, leaning in closer to Mum, the top half of my body and head lying next to hers. She felt so soft, jelly-like. I whispered some mantras I use to calm myself down at night when anxiety grabs hold of me. I said them for her, but they helped me too.

"I am calm."

"I am safe."

"I am supported."

I repeated these words slowly, over and over, into Mum's ear for 10 minutes or more, aware that dawn was about to break. I could hear the birds and see a dim light from the sun, which had been mainly hidden by clouds for days, starting to fill the room. I continued with my mantras and watched Jude, Sam, and Mum sleep. I remembered the delirium caused by the combination of lack of sleep and stress when I had my babies. I was reminded of lying awake at this time of the morning and how hard I found that time in my life, but also how much I missed my kids being babies. I apologised to Nanna and thought about her and Dadda and about how I didn't really think of them as much as I should. For some reason, I had always thought more about my Uncle Michael over the years. I spoke to all of them in my head, thanking them for everything they had done for me and everything they would do for Mum. I thanked Mum. I told her what a great job she had done as my mum, Sam's mum, and as a grandmother to our kids, and how much I appreciated her depth and authenticity.

She was such a "real person". She wasn't "amazing" the way that everybody apparently is these days. She just always did her best, with the little that she had in an external sense, to be a great mother and a nice person. I watched the room slowly get brighter and realised I was busting for the toilet.

The room was so quiet aside from the constant sound of Mum, Sam, and Jude snoring — so, not quiet at all really, but any tiny noise I made to extract myself from the small space I was in, propped up on two chairs, seemed to be loud enough that I was worried I would wake them. I was taken back to the tension and ordeal of trying to keep my babies asleep while sliding weightlessly out of their room, remembering with a smile the stealth superpowers I had developed to achieve this on the odd, exhilarating occasion.

I lifted my body weight with my hands on the arms of the chair, swinging my legs wide, ninja style, landing feet together like a sparrow on the ground. I had a little chuckle to myself as I tiptoed, prancing lightly off to the bathroom and made the decision to flush the toilet later rather than take the risk of waking anyone, as I had done all those years ago while my babies finally slept. I managed, due to my intense training back then, to get back into my spot somehow, barely making a peep, keeping everyone asleep.

I enjoyed that time there with everyone, on my own. I had been on quite the emotional rollercoaster, as they say, over the course of that night, and it was nice to come out the other side having a little laugh with myself and a peaceful start to the day, for once.

Chapter 6 – Bubbles

The next day was day three in palliative care. It felt like so much longer, so I can only imagine how Mum must have felt, which I don't really like to do, since she had been going through it for longer than we knew. The weather was changing, although there were still rainy patches. Despite our awareness of the lockdown in the outside world, we hadn't given it much thought. It was as though we were existing on a different planet, and that kind of information seemed irrelevant. A lot had happened in those 24 hours of our lives. Sam and Jude were both maintaining contact with the outside world, discovering that masks were required if you went into public places such as supermarkets or restaurants. Mask mandates had not been a requirement of any of the lockdown processes Queensland had gone through prior to this. But as I was the only one to have not even gone back out to reception, let alone leave the hospital grounds, it had zero impact on my life as I cruised between the tearoom, our ensuite, and Mum's bedside.

We also learnt that there had been protests and shootings in Washington. Good old Donald, helped along by his mate Rupert, had incited a mental mass mob to form, and shots had been fired inside the Capitol Building. The world was going crazy for us, but for lots of other people, too, it seemed. I deliberately didn't seek further details. I had enough on my plate, but it made me realise, in perhaps a disturbing way, that inside my bubble of watching and waiting for my mum to die, I felt sheltered; at times even happy, protected from all the noise and nonsense that happens in the "real world".

Things were hard in that bubble. I had no control. Things were unfolding that I didn't want to be happening. But somehow, perhaps because I was surrounded by so much love and such a depth of emotion, experiencing connection, authenticity, and joy, it almost felt like a break. That "break" had taken me into another reality that had its own challenges, but oddly, was a nicer place to be. I can be so overwhelmed by all the potential things that could go wrong in my life, mainly related to the kids — people can be so scary and cruel, someone could hurt them, or they could get sick, that kind of thing. During those few days, and for many months that would follow, my "normal" negative thoughts stopped. It was like the experience was cleansing. Sharing the privilege of watching Mum die was such a profound gift that every other focus faded away. I was experiencing the "reality" of life through death. A gateway into the "real world". Spending that time with her, despite the horror and desperation that I also experienced, created a sense of stillness within me, and I am certain that she played a hand in that.

Although not a fully considered decision, I had not yet told anyone in my life aside from family who already knew what had happened and what was going on. I just didn't have the energy for it. Aside from making calls to Ev, I felt more respectful of the process to stay off my phone and didn't want to have to respond to messages for updates or even support purposes. I wanted to be present, focused solely on Mum.

Jude was doing a great and necessary job of communicating with our family, which was of primary importance, and I hadn't gotten to the "tell your friends" module yet, preferring to just sink into the intensity of our connection within the bubble, and not have to infiltrate my life with anything other than what was happening in this alternative universe.

Despite this, I realised it had been my friend Mel's birthday the day before, and I wanted to acknowledge that, so that made me decide it was as good a time as any to start that module. Mel's mum had died about nine months earlier after a very sad and long battle with dementia. After calling her, I rang my friend Tan, asking her to pass the news on to our friends in common. With that job started at least, I responded to text messages from family, and called Ev for an update from my end and to get one from his. Aside from these interactions, it was Sam and Jude who were maintaining contact with the outside world for communication and supply purposes.

By now, we had met quite a few nurses. Courts had a new partner, who was also young but didn't seem to have the same level of experience with nursing palliative people and, therefore, interacting with their families as she did. He didn't initially get a name from us, but would eventually come to be known as "Mr Unaware" for reasons that may not be as straightforward as you might think. There was also a Pommie nurse, probably in her mid-fifties, who spoke with a northern accent. We named her Mrs Tiddywinkles because she reminded Sam of a character from Peter Rabbit, who we now know to be called Mrs Tiggy-Winkle, who is actually a kind old hedgehog who does everyone's laundry. In this Peter Rabbit character mix-up, the hedgehog was in stark contrast, because he certainly did not see the nurse this way; he found her extremely annoying, more like a "bossy boots" type of character. (I've since googled Peter Rabbit characters, and still don't know what he was on about with that). Maybe that's harsh, but hey, he's entitled to his opinion!

Kate was still around from time to time, thankfully, but we hadn't seen the leprechaun since first arriving, which was a shame. We'd met another nurse we'd christened "Michael's girlfriend". She was a bit rough with her approach towards both Mum and us. Her blunt explanations where jarring given our fragile state, and her loud voice and overall demeanour contrasted with what we had gotten used to with the much softer Courts. We'd settled on "Michael's girlfriend" because Jude thought she'd be someone her ex-husband might date.

Our introduction to her was also less than ideal — she was the one who bumped into Sam's leg when things had first taken a big turn with the secretions, giving us the impression that his presence by his dying mother's bedside was a nuisance to her. Despite all of this, we came to realise that there was also kindness, under her gruff exterior. Mum, Jude, Sam, and I were "the gang" amidst this supporting cast of nurses. We all had our roles to play, and all good stories have light and shade. In that way, all of these personalities, these "characters" in the story, bonded us and helped us manage or laugh our way through each "scene".

The morning was spent making phone calls and wiping away the secretions in between each drain, like it was no big deal. We had become so accustomed to this new lifestyle that this "stuff" had lost its hold over us, becoming more like changing your baby's nappy and having no big reaction to doing so, regardless of what mess you come across. That's a horrible analogy, but it's true. Both bodily processes are unpleasant, but you become desensitised. Especially when it relates to someone you love, you move on, and you don't mind. You quickly build an immunity and stop being confronted by it. If you don't, it interferes with caring for the person with respect.

Sam and I had a chuckle at how bizarre our lives had become. Engrossed in our conversation as we sat on either side of Mum, wiping her nose and face clean, we realised we'd gone through two boxes of tissues as bloody, snotty tissues were piling up everywhere. Later that day, the three of us were sitting around Mum chatting, and her gurgling was so loud that we couldn't hear each other. It was as if it were background noise, even though it was so pervasive. We had to keep raising our voices, not consciously noticing we were shouting. Sam, without realising he was irritated by not being able to hear the conversation, looked down and sternly said

"Shush, Mum."

With a quick pause in conversation and a *look* at each other, we all cracked up (this memory is cracking me up even now as I write this). Shushing your death-rattling mother because she's dying so loudly that you can't chat over her motionless body may seem very insensitive, but that was how it was; funny like that, if you get that kind of dark humour we share. Without those moments (and there were many of them), it wouldn't be the treasured time and memory that it was and is. Such a textured experience of the gamut of all emotions. A story of the mother I love dying a slow death, and how I've never laughed and cried so much in all my life.

It was slow, but because of that, it was meaningful. She did things slowly, so it was death done her way, and although I am certain she was so relieved when it was over, I believe that she wouldn't change it. Pain and laughter were her life, and as it turned out, her death. Profound and hilarious — that was her style. Sometimes at the same time, sometimes on purpose, sometimes without meaning to be, but that was her style. Everything and nothing was sacred in that bubble we had formed.

A good example of the nothing aspect was the day the death rattles started. We discussed the possibility that this could go on for quite some time. If that was the case, we decided it might be a good idea if Sam and I said goodbye to Mum and quietly slipped into the bathroom so Jude could smother her with a pillow, which sent us into stitches of laughter. Now that may seem a little harsh for most "normal people", but it's one of our favourite parts of the story. It enabled us to cope. It made the experience "us". We were okay because we were all so in tune with each other that we could make a joke like that and use laughter as a reprieve, even if it was at a plan to do away with her because we (including presumably Mum) had all had enough.

Times like those, jokes and laughter like that, kept us going and made us stronger, and we knew Mum would be laughing too if she could. We shared that brand of humour, so we used it as the asset that it was and always will be. We laughed so often and so hard that sometimes we wondered if they could hear us in the corridor. We guessed they would assume that the noise was crying or wailing, rather than us pissing ourselves laughing so crazily at such a time, so often.

Presumably, bedside vigils are usually a lot more sombre. Perhaps they were thinking what an emotional family we were. It was horrific, of course. Our hearts were breaking, but I have such deep gratitude for the laughter we shared. I was in no way isolated by my sense of humour, which I have always felt to be one of my strongest assets.

What a blessing it was to share that with my other "gang members", to be able to spend such a time wiping away just as many tears caused by laughter as by sadness. The magic was always there because we allowed feelings to flow. We weren't trapped or silenced by our fear, sorrow, or jokes. We supported each other. No one was getting it wrong or right. We did Mum, Nanna, and Dadda proud by laughing and crying *together* the whole time, loving and respecting each other *as a family*, as it should be.

Sam went to get some lunch and was made aware, despite no one saying anything to any of us prior, that we were supposed to be wearing masks "at all times", not just at the shops. None of us had been doing so, so it could therefore be assumed that no one mentioning it meant that no one was concerned. The only people we were interacting with, albeit in a limited way, were medical staff, who had started wearing masks, leading us to the logical assumption that it was a medical directive, so we thought nothing of it. We eventually also learnt that the rule also applied even when we were in our room. We understood the need for precautions and had been following the rules as we understood them to be, but this felt a bit much, given our breaking hearts and lack of sleep. We complied for the most part, not wanting to make an issue of it. We did not have a reference point of having to wear masks before, and were spending long periods on our own anyway, so we assumed that only meant we also needed to wear them if we left the room. To sit there with them on when it was just the four of us seemed completely pointless.

We were having some lunch, and Mrs Tiddywinkles came in and instantly snapped at us for not having a mask on. We were all quite perplexed, wondering how we were supposed to eat while wearing a mask. She told us we had to eat outside, even though the door to the courtyard was locked. I hadn't considered leaving the room just to eat, let alone walking through the building to get out there. Despite the rule having only been vaguely mentioned to us a short time earlier, it had apparently been in force for well over 24 hours. She wasn't having any of our "nonsense" when we tried explaining this, ordering us to put our masks on at once!

Our comprehension or experiences of mask wearing are vastly different since it went on to become "the norm", but her attitude really rubbed Sam, in particular, the wrong way, especially since he was already not a fan. It felt like an assault on our peace and quiet. She refused to acknowledge the legitimate reasons we had for making this "massive breach of protocol", despite us making it clear that we weren't arguing about the rule, as much as we were upset by her tone.

Now, while I have said that Sam has a level head, by contrast, he also has a bad temper, which can flare up in the blink of an eye. He continued to try to put forth his position, mainly that we were eating and didn't really want to leave Mum to have to do so, and that we hadn't even had the rules explained. But Mrs Tiddywinkles remained firm with her stance, saying that if Sam didn't stop talking, didn't put his mask on, and if that she caught any of us, anywhere, ever again not wearing our masks, she was going to "escalate" us which we took to mean "dob" on us and possibly have us removed from the room or grounds. The thought of being kicked out and potentially having a situation where Mum would be left behind to die on her own, with only Mrs Tiddywinkles of all people for company, filled me with anxiety. Sam and Jude, however, whilst irritated, seemed to think she was a joke, but with what I felt was on the line, I insisted to Sam that he shut up.

We sat quietly outside the curtain around Mum's bed while Mrs Tiddywinkles and Kate assisted her, Sam sarcastically pretending to try to eat his sandwich with his mask on. We were all not functioning at our best capacity, including, unfortunately, Mrs Tiddywinkles.

Despite this, I was happy to put Mrs Tiddywinkles' complete lack of bedside manner down to the possibility that, being from England, she knew people who had suffered with and perhaps died of COVID, so was likely to be more stressed about the rules than us and perhaps even the other Australian medical staff. I also understand that being palliative, doesn't mean that it doesn't matter if you get COVID; in fact, you would be more susceptible to it, and this would have a potentially disastrous flow-on effect within the hospital system, let alone the potential outcomes for that patient.

Regardless of what we were all thinking, feeling, and insisting, this wasn't a good part of the story for us. The fear of being told to leave, whether likely or not, was more than enough for me to follow her request and try to calm Sam and, to a lesser extent, Jude down, even though I agreed that it seemed to be a ridiculous rule. But as is Sam's way, and apparently, as was hers, the getting the last word in battle between him and Mrs Tiddywinkles continued, until I finally managed to pull Sam's head in. Shortly afterwards, Kate came back by herself. She let us know that she supported her colleague but also understood our predicament, and was happy to leave the application of the "masks on in the room rule" up to us. She said she would try to check on Mum's needs a little more often on her own, so that we could have a bit more "privacy". As I said earlier, Kate was beautiful.

At some stage that day, we began discussing funeral arrangements, flicking through the little booklet they'd left us, *What to Do When Someone Dies*. It advises getting funeral preparations underway ASAP. We laughed about how strange it felt to be doing so while Mum was still lying there, in earshot, hanging on with every inch of her being. We thought we'd at least try to figure out which funeral director to use. Logically, that's one of the first steps, according to the book. Apparently, it is best if you can "make a reservation". Although Jude had been down this road before, she hadn't done so in Queensland, so she had no idea where to start either. I contacted Mel, who had had a bad experience with a company in the area, to at least rule one out, but aside from that, Jude and I believed they were pretty much all the same, sincere on some level perhaps, but primarily driven by money, nonetheless. Perhaps that's a harsh way to see it, but we figured that is just the way it is when it comes to the funeral industry.

Sam, usually the sceptic among the three of us, wasn't so convinced that we should just pick a name out of the hat, so he started researching options. We discussed using Drysdale Funerals, only because we thought we remembered an ad on TV with Wally Lewis singing their praises. Mum was not a fan, by any stretch, of Wally. Sam and Jude felt the same way, whereas I, being the only Queenslander among us, quite liked this idea. Mainly because the imagery of Mum being lowered into the ground by Wally Lewis tickled my funny bone, especially given how much she used to whinge about him.

For some reason, whatever indiscretions Sam believed he had had on the field, he seemed to be going along with the idea that Wally wouldn't put his name to such a thing without a genuine reason. With Jude and me insisting that we needed to lock something in, particularly as I was keen to tick at least something off our very long list, Drysdale's almost got the nod. We worked out a few weeks later that it was actually George Hartnett that Wally was spruiking, so choosing Drysdale based on his recommendation would've been quite a balls-up!

Sam was unwavering in his quest to find the perfect combination of ethics and care at a reasonable cost. He was determined to find a non-franchised, family-run, or small business enterprise, not affiliated with big corporate companies that are more concerned with shareholders than the customer experience, so the service provided would possibly be more sincere. Before long, Jude and I realised it was best to leave him to his devices, or device literally, while he continued his research mission.

All three of us like to think that we throw a good party and are organised in varying degrees, but Sam is *very* driven when it comes to event coordination. We could see that finding the perfect company, even if Jude and I didn't think it was possible to do so, was important to him. I was happy that he took over that department anyway. I was enjoying the fact that I still didn't have to be on my phone and use my brain in that way. Doing so made room to receive messages I felt I was getting, as though they were being placed in my brain from somewhere in the ether, such as that the poem, *I Hold Your Heart in my Heart*, should be included somehow in the funeral. I remembered it being read at a friend's wedding many years ago, and although I really couldn't recall much more than the title, I received the message from whoever sent it, making a mental note to investigate further.

We also started (of course) to discuss music for the funeral. We were excited yet overwhelmed by the enormous importance of getting this aspect right for Mum, but just as much for ourselves. In perhaps a freaky "coincidence", Jude shared a conversation she and Mum had had only one week earlier while shopping together at Bunnings. For no particular reason, Mum started talking about good songs for funerals, telling Jude that *Eagle When She Flies* by Dolly Parton would be a really good one. At the time, they chuckled about this being a weird conversation to have in the plumbing aisle, but also acknowledged that it was relatively normal for our family.

Sam and I were excited because we'd never heard it, strange that it hadn't crossed our paths, given that we, in part, come from a long line of country music lovers. Jude told us it was an excellent song, but more to the point, how perfect it was for Mum.

We agreed to lock it in, deliberating whether we should listen to it then and there, but decided to be patient and wait until after Mum had died. The timing, again, timing is everything, of them having that discussion only days earlier, added to the magic that talking about music creates, but in particular, music used to represent a person on the occasion of their funeral. We were buzzing with anticipation of selecting the funeral soundtrack, and the fact that Mum had already chosen the title track helped to lift our mood even higher.

Sam told a story about how for years, Kel had raved about a chicken burger, chips, and gravy she used to get growing up in her hometown, and how when Sam had finally tried them, they didn't live up to Kel's hype or his expectation. That type of scenario had gone down in their history books and was known between them as a "Super Rooster Moment" — referencing the name of the shop. We hoped that *Eagle When She Flies* wasn't going to be a Super Rooster Moment when Sam and I listened to it.

With no other conclusions or funeral homes contacted, the afternoon was setting in, so we decided to pass the time by listening to some tunes and having another drink. It was Saturday, so another Guinness was probably the right thing to do. We pulled the curtain around Mum's bed to give us a bit of a buffer if "someone" were to come in, our masks handy. The obvious problem with having a party adhering to the regulations was that Mum couldn't head outside with us. Going out there to party without her seemed a bit wrong, even for us three, who had joked about smothering her with a pillow, so we cranked the tunes and cracked a can from inside the new bubble, within our wider bubble, with an awareness that this was a different vibe to the "send-off" we'd had the afternoon before. We discussed that Mum was going to do this in her own time and that this session was not about giving her marching orders (although we weren't insisting that she stay). It was just a chilled, quiet Saturday afternoon drink with friends.

The rain had stopped, and there was a nice cool breeze in the air, so for the first time since we had "checked in", we opened the window and the back door, now that Mrs Tiddywinkles had arranged for it to be unlocked. It was so nice to have everything open, free flowing — released. Mum had a nice, gentle wind and filtered sunlight sweeping over her. The clouds had cleared, the rain had left its sparkles, and everything felt very energised. It felt like the room itself was being "washed out", refreshing us all. I lifted the sheets off Mum's legs so her arms, face and legs could be touched by the breeze.

We had a drink, we laughed and talked about the old days and shared our funny family stories. It was a relaxed mingling-at-a-cocktail-party style of afternoon. I even went for a little wander, finally venturing out to explore the courtyard and gardens. Finding a chair under a hedge around the corner from Mum's room, I took the opportunity to finally call Dad back, after several missed calls and text messages that Sam hadn't responded to. We didn't intend for him to feel disregarded. He and I spoke for a little while, and I tried my best to put his needlessly, yet reasonably so, worried mind at ease.

I rang Ev for another update and had a chat with the girls. They thought Mimi still being alive was a good thing, so I agreed, but made certain that they did understand that didn't mean she was coming home. Ev informed me that our cat, Lexi, had been unwell since the night we had all left for the hospital. She was bad enough that he had taken her to the vet. She was very stressed about something and was unable to control her bladder and was weeing everywhere. The test they did was inconclusive, but she was on medication in lieu of doing nothing, requiring Ev to first catch her, then hold her down to administer it, which was distressing to everyone, including obviously Lexi.

He had covered all the furniture with sheets and towels and was using chairs to try to barricade the beds. This behaviour was totally out of character for Lexi. We figured it could be anxiety, caused by me yelling and us all leaving so suddenly. We joked that Lexi always seemed to really like Mum, so she was probably upset by what was happening to her, and how Sam's cat, McGarnagle, didn't seem to care in the slightest that Mum was dying. Clearly, Lexi was Mum's favourite of the two grand-cats, in the same way that I was the favourite of her two children.

After my calls, I stayed outside in my corner, closed my eyes, and purposefully absorbed the early evening breeze on my face and arms. I could smell the salt air from the nearby Redcliffe Esplanade. I felt abundance. I was appreciative of the gifts of Mum not dying alone and all that we were sharing as a family. I felt as though I would, from then on, be able to handle anything, that I had been transformed. I was excited by the possibilities that this new version of my life would create for me. Although I was so drained, I also felt so strong and so positive.

After a nice amount of time alone, I went back inside. We discussed and agreed that if Mum were to keep hanging on for another few days, we did in fact have emotional reserves to manage individually and as a support to each other. We accepted that nothing was going to change if it wasn't time for it to. If Mum was comfortable, this wasn't all that bad after all. What's not to like? We get to have a drink occasionally, talk shit to each other all day and night, and listen to whatever music we want. It really could be worse.

With the afternoon on its way out again for another day, we continued to relax and make the most of our time together, in particular, our time with Mum, for however long it would last. Courts was back, with Mr "Yet to Be Named", as our third night approached. Although I had been picking at food, I was barely eating. I had not yet had a proper meal, a sandwich even, since lunch at home the day we found Mum, so when Sam returned from getting us some dinner, with a selection of delicious-smelling Asian dishes, I was salivating. I hadn't realised until then that I felt like I was starving. It also occurred to me that I still wasn't even drinking water, only the occasional tea, coffee, and Guinness. It was around 6 o'clock, and the air was cool with the hint of more rain on the way. The three of us — masks on (we were now referring to ourselves as "The Three Maskateers") — piled our plates from the delectable choices and started making our way outside, leaving the nurses to attend to Mum.

Standing just by the door, we realised something was happening behind the curtain. Mum was making some horrible noises, and we could hear loud whispering, although we couldn't make out what was being said. Suddenly, another nurse rushed in, then Courts came out from behind the curtain, reassuring us that everything was fine, yet bolted out of the room as if there was an emergency. Mr "Yet to Be Named" and the other nurse, I think it was "Michael's girlfriend", seemed to be arguing, or sounded at the very least stressed. It was clear that something was wrong.

Again, this is another scene in the story that doesn't seem to make sense, given how much we love our mum and sister and the level to which we were busting ourselves to ensure she was given the best possible care by us, and the staff, but there was a certain part of my brain that was so desperately needing food. I had a whole plate full of it, my favourite food, right there under my nose, and had already set my intentions and focus on providing my body and well-being with this fuel. But after all my pleading, after all the times I just needed it to be over and all the emphasis on Mum being comfortable, not in pain, not scared, which it now sounded like she might be feeling, I couldn't help but think:

Not now, don't die now, Mum.

Not now, nurses. After all the great care, why does it have to be now that you are fucking things up? Maybe making her die and therefore stopping me from enjoying this meal?

Retrospectively, I see how my exhaustion and lack of food and water were impacting me. The prolonged experience was making me almost disassociate from reality at times, and although I intellectually understood what was going on, there were times like this one, when I didn't really believe any of it was really happening.

So, there we stood, dumbfounded, wondering what we could or should do, when all we really could do was watch on, feeling anxiety and physical tension, but mostly, what I was feeling was hungry.

Courts raced back in, joining the others. Blocked from knowing what was happening by the hushed voices and curtain, we stood in the doorway slowly eating our dinner, stunned, glancing at each other with confused but satisfied looks on our faces. We couldn't rush in behind that curtain. We wanted to stay out of the way and not cause a distraction or take focus away from whatever needed to be done to help Mum. There wasn't even an opportunity to ask questions. Was this *it*? We didn't know what to make of it, or do, so we just waited, slowly eating. Trying (not that it was hard because it was delicious), to enjoy the taste and the feeling of having something substantial going into my belly. Desensitised perhaps by so long watching and waiting for Mum to die, so institutionalised by medical procedures that we just kept on eating, and whatever was happening went on long enough for me to almost finish my meal.

The male nurse came out, leaving the others attending to Mum, and ushered us further into the dimly lit courtyard. He was white. His whole body, his hands, and even his eyeballs, it seemed, were visibly shaking. He looked as though he was petrified, like he'd seen a ghost, which I did wonder at the time, was possibly not just a metaphor. His voice was trembling as he tried to gather himself and act professional enough to tell us what had happened. He provided us with a very convoluted explanation that told us nothing. Something had happened during the draining process, which was obvious, as to what, to this day, we do not know (despite ordering the medical record file from the hospital two years later, which shed no light).

Our concern in that moment was more focused on this guy than it was on Mum or on ourselves. His distress made us uneasy about pressing him for clearer information. We knew there was no ill intention from the staff. Every nurse had been very caring towards Mum, but something happened, maybe a mistake, which we all as humans make on occasion in our workplaces. That is our best guess. Of course, we had an expectation that he was ensuring Mum was comfortable, let alone his actual duty to make sure she was, but we could see that he was extremely upset by whatever had happened, so we didn't bombard him and exacerbate his agitation. I distinctly remember stroking his arm, squeezing his shoulder and telling him to slow his breathing; it was okay.

He told us that Mum would have been fine throughout whatever had happened, despite her sounding to the contrary. He said she was "totally unaware" and "didn't have any idea what was going on around her", which we felt was quite insulting. The fact that he seemed so sure, without ever having been in Mum's position, obviously, or having validation from anyone who had been, was also annoying. But we let that go too. "Mr Unaware" now had a name at least, and it worked on more than one level. However, in the days, months, and years afterwards, our distress, maybe also our busy body curiosity, intensified. We would all love to know what it was that went on behind that curtain. Yet again, perhaps it is best that we do not. Later that evening, Courts tried her best to provide an explanation. Regardless, we still didn't understand, either because we were too tired, or it wasn't explained well, on purpose or otherwise, but eventually we were left on our own again.

Mum was better, so we decided it was best to leave the stress behind us and move forward into the night, onto whatever was next, whatever "modules" we still needed to pass.

Back gathered as our gang, we laughed about the funny things that had happened so far and debriefed about the traumatic side of the experience we were having. Jude shared the similarities of Nanna's dying story, although that was a two-week-long version of what we were going through. Jude told us that she had eventually reached such a level of exhaustion that she told (unconscious) Nanna that she couldn't wait any longer and started packing her belongings to go home, hoping that her attempt at "tough love" would get Nanna "over the line". We wondered if Jude's experience with Nanna might hold a few clues. Why would Mum want to go anywhere when we were having such a good time being together? Not only the parties, but the day-to-day goings on. We were in this profound yet hilarious experience, for the longest amount of uninterrupted time we had probably ever spent together. Maybe, like us, she was having a good time, in amongst the pain and suffering, because she was being so well supported and loved so ferociously. As sad as it is to admit, she didn't get that kind of love very often.

Her grandchildren had all, from time to time and at different stages of their lives, given her that depth of regard and feeling of unconditional expectation, but the three of us hadn't since we were little kids ourselves, when we were her little sister, her little girl, and little boy. Maybe she was hanging on to feel that for as long as she could.

Jude suggested it was also perhaps that she didn't want to leave Sam and me again. When Mum and Dad separated when we were kids, we stayed living with Dad in our family home. The plan was for Mum to get settled elsewhere, as it was more practical for Dad to stay for work reasons, and once she had done so, we would then live with her. In the meantime, in the blink of an eye, Dad found a new partner. She had no children of her own, but had always wanted them, and a custody battle commenced. The years that Mum lived separately from us broke her heart (was that one of the "everything I've ever done to you" things that Dad had apologised for? Did he have enough insight for that one?). She had honestly never fully recovered from the years spent mothering us from afar, with constant obstructions from our stepmother and, to some extent, our father.

    We also discussed that perhaps what was happening was the opposite. Mum had lived alone for so many years. She had learnt, as sad as I am to say, to make loneliness her normal, to cope with it, despite wishing things could be different. She enjoyed her own company but would have also loved to have had more direct contact with Sam and me, and to have had more friends. But maybe this was too much for her? A "culture shock" — too overwhelming? She hadn't spent a single second alone since Sam had found her. Was that resulting in her not being able to really take the time and have the space she needed to set herself free? Perhaps an element of both things could be true. We knew for certain that rushing her didn't do any of us any favours, but these other two perspectives were interesting, if not useful. Whether Mum was staying deliberately because she didn't want to leave, or because she just hadn't figured out how to yet, we were beginning to get to a point where we were releasing some of our expectations, making it easier to relax into the impending night. We were well on our way to completing Module 2.98, "Don't force the process".

***

We decided to tidy up a bit before settling down for the night. My stuff was spread out everywhere, so I started organising my mess. There was a small butterfly magnet made from thin plastic for the wings, which had been above Mum's bed from the time we arrived. I had been joking since then that I was going to steal it when we left, because I am the family thief (another one of those well-used family jokes).

    Despite having no idea how long the road ahead was or what we would still encounter on it, I decided it was time to nab it as my memento. Perhaps I was trying to give Mum the impression we were packing up to leave, but with a bit more subtlety than Jude's approach with Nanna. I placed the magenta and blue butterfly into my bag with my rose quartz, and we settled into our spots again, prepared as best as possible for whatever lay ahead for us. Jude was on the bed, Sam and I on either side of Mum. We continued chatting but mostly sat in silent reflection.

Without specifically discussing a new directive, maybe because of our earlier talk about Mum possibly feeling a bit smothered, we were less intent on abiding by our "don't leave Mum alone" rule. We'd heard those stories about someone dying as soon as their loved ones left the room. We weren't deliberately leaving her to make that happen, but we did what we needed to do without being as concerned about who was whereas we had been previously. It was the quietest, easiest night. We felt calm. We had surrendered.

Jude was on her phone, and Sam and I had our heads on Mum's bed. The lights were dim. We hadn't called it a night officially, but were winding down, ready for another night in our bubble. I realised that the severe bursitis I had in my left shoulder had not troubled me at all since arriving, despite all the weird and uncomfortable sleeping and sitting positions I had been in. It had been such a big part of my life for the past two months, giving me daily bouts of agonising pain, and I found the absence of it, as well as my unawareness of the absence of it until then, a genuine miracle. I remember thanking the universe for taking that little part of the puzzle out for me to allow me to focus on everything else and not have my own physical pain be a part of the story.

We sat in peace. In recalling this night as I recall it now, I realise that I still hadn't contemplated my life without Mum in it. It was the dying that I was so focused on, not the "being dead forever" part. I hadn't imagined how my life would look and feel without her physically being here. I wasn't up to that "module" yet, I suppose.

Chapter 7 – Despair

I'm writing this one year on from the night my mum went to bed in her little home for the last time.

I realise now that maybe the dread I have been feeling for weeks leading up to what was our last Christmas together, the turning of the new year, and the first anniversary of her death, is linked to this part of the story, more so than the part about her dying and being dead for a whole year. I can see her in my mind's eye as my mum, who was getting old. Her hair was white, her arms were soft, wrinkly like my nanna's used to be. My beautiful Mum, whom I used to put very little effort into, in all honesty, yet I'd be irritated by the worry and anxiety I felt when I thought about her being on her own. I am recalling the guilt I felt about being of very little practical help and in some ways emotional help to her, but regardless, rarely put much action into alleviating. Instead, I just continued to feel annoyed, as if my feeling guilty was also *her* fault in some way.

I'm imagining her having her shower that night. Sometimes she had a shower in the morning, but it was summer, so I'm sure she would have had one that night as well, then maybe she did something on her laptop, or channel surfed on the TV. She wouldn't have had a cup of tea, I don't think, because she wasn't really one to do that before bed, although I know there were nights when she couldn't sleep, so would get up and make herself one. I feel it's likely that she was in a relaxed mood that night. We had all spent a nice Christmas together, and her diary entries around that time were very positive. Or perhaps on that night, now nine days since our great Christmas and eight days since last talking to me, was she feeling lonely again? Deflated that after such a lovely time, things had gone back to normal, and she was alone again, as usual.

She had spoken to Orla on New Year's Day on Orla's first mobile phone, a Christmas gift. Mimi was the first person she'd called on it. They had a nice long chat, but I didn't get on at the end to say Happy New Year, or even hello. I was "too busy".

I was lying in my bed tonight, trying to calm my heavy grief, focusing on my soft and comfortable pillow, and how safe I was in my bed. Unable to unwind, I decided to get up to write about this moment in time as it stands for me right now, imagining Mum on this night last year sorting out her CPAP machine and hopping into her bed. Settling in and, hopefully, feeling the softness of her pillow, the safety of her surroundings. Even though I, of course, hope that she was comfortable and at peace with her world, it almost makes it harder to bear the thought that she had no knowledge of what was coming at her. She had no idea that tomorrow night and the next night, and late into the afternoon of the day after, she would be lying on her hard kitchen floor, sometimes in pain, always uncomfortable and alone, feeling very unsafe.

Would she be dreaming of her soft pillow and cosy bed? Pleading for it?

There's no doubt she would be begging for someone to rescue her. How long did she spend in shock? How much pain did she feel initially, let alone as the days progressed? How often was she awake, how often was she conscious? Did she hear my first phone call? Did she hear my second and third phone calls and my text notifications? What was she telling herself? Was she wanting it to be over, or was she trying hard to stay alive? Did she have any moments during that terrifying, desperate, drawn-out time where she felt peace?

We'll never know these answers, and by the time we see her again, I don't think those things will be of importance in that place, so we may never know. But we do know she needed help, and she had to wait so long for it to arrive. She had no idea on this night that she would have such a long struggle ahead. A struggle to try to undress herself. A struggle to lie in her own bodily fluids, either because she didn't even realise she had been incontinent, or worse, that she did and had to endure the struggle and distress of not being able to get herself to the toilet. She would have to just lie there and let that happen and get it all through her hair and soak her body to the point where it would take days before she could smell clean.

She didn't know that she would probably also be struggling to breathe, if not for the lack of oxygen flowing freely because of her trauma, but also from her dry throat that would eventually, presumably, make swallowing a struggle. She didn't know any of this, and I know I'm probably just in a moment now, but somehow in this moment, that almost makes it feel worse, like she was a precious innocent little child who didn't know that tomorrow was going to unleash the biggest physical and emotional battle of her lifetime.

I desperately want to travel back in time to call her! I want to warn her! If I can't change any of it, I feel like it would be fairer if she at least knew what was going to happen, but I also don't want her to know. How would I ever be able to tell her that? Would that make it better or worse? Really, what I want is for her to drift easily off to sleep, on her soft, comfortable bed and wake up tomorrow feeling happy, refreshed, and at peace with her world. If I can't change the outcome of any of it, what I would love to be able to do is call her to tell her I love her more than anything in the wide world and that I'm sorry for not telling her that enough, and for fighting against her so often for no reason. I'm so sorry for making her feel any less than the most beautiful, most open-hearted, kindest person I know.

Instead of calling her in a day's time to suggest we go for lunch next week, I want to call her *now* and tell her I'll catch the train down in the morning, and we'll go for lunch, which I know she would be delighted about. Then I'd have certainty she'd be going to bed feeling pleased and positive, and then she wouldn't have a massive stroke and heart attack alone in her kitchen sometime after 1:49 p.m. tomorrow and have to lie on the floor and endure what she endured, leaving so many questions to try not to contemplate the answers to.

Even if the outcome was still that she had a massive stroke and heart attack, and, maybe even if she still died, I could reconcile that if the context of it was different, compared to the thought of her lying alone on her hard floor, in agony, hot, thirsty, uncomfortable, and scared for two days and two nights.

I'm so sorry we took so long, Mum.

Good night. Sleep tight. See you in the morning light.

Chapter 8 – Synergy

Getting to this part of the story is a strange place to be. The story is about my mum dying, so it was inevitably going to arrive here after all the moments, big and small, that came before. Interesting to others, maybe not, but included regardless, for my own self-indulgent need to record everything because it is all important to me.

The most formative few days of my life.

I never want to forget all the details that made it so special. But now I am at this part, it feels like a bit of an anticlimax, in writing about it at least. Like, there's less of a story when it comes to what happened next. Bad for writing purposes, but the experience of it, where there was really nothing to talk about or think about, was just as magical as any of the other moments. A surprise ending after all the spinning, falling, leaping, and flying that we had done in the time beforehand.

This is the part where she dies.

***

We were physically drained but feeling at ease, and the energy of the room was peaceful. Mum had recently had a drain and was just making her "usual" sounds as we rested in silence. It was getting late, and we were close to calling it a night.

Slowly but surely, we began to sense something; we all felt it, acknowledging it with a look at each other. Mum's breathing started sounding slightly different, but that wasn't our only cue. We *felt her* change. We sensed that she was packing her things, getting ready to go. This time, she didn't have to worry about getting out to her car before realising she'd left her keys or laptop inside, as was so often the case when she'd come for visits. It felt like she was taking a long, deep breath in, as you'd do before something exhilarating like jumping off a waterfall, but she hardly moved; it wasn't a sense of adrenaline as such. *Something just changed in the air,* and we felt it.

Sam and I sat across from each other staring with a combination of somehow knowing exactly what was happening, whilst also wondering if this was just another of her "false alarm pranks". We knew it wasn't, but we didn't trust what we knew, perhaps because we subconsciously weren't ready to accept it, or were in a subtle state of shock, probably both, but after a few minutes, we fell into the belief. Mum was telling us, without doing anything other than lying there peacefully, telling herself, maybe too, that it was time.

We signalled to Jude in quiet reverence, but with almost a smile on our faces, that we would give her the exact moment it happened so she could record the time. Despite not having discussed it, the three of us knew what the signal was about. We wanted to know her exact time of death, for astrological charting purposes that we would never actually need, but we wanted to record it for Mum. It was well known how annoyed she had always been that she didn't know her exact time of birth. It made mapping her chart difficult because she couldn't pinpoint it with accuracy, so in a silly way, we figured knowing her exact time of death might bring her some closure on that. We were almost more focused on getting that right over the fact that, after all the lead-up, she was finally going to die.

Suddenly, there was a knock at the door and a nurse we hadn't met let herself in before we could respond. The room was dimly lit, so her eyes wouldn't have adjusted quickly enough to assess the scene, and besides, it looked as though nothing much was happening. Jude was closest to her and whispered that we were okay, giving her a firm hint that we wanted to be alone. She didn't seem to be getting the memo and just kept talking to Jude, who, while being polite, was making it very clear that this was a private time and was asking her to leave, whilst simultaneously trying to maintain focus on what was happening with Mum.

The nurse finally registered what was happening and left. We had a little laugh about her timing and how sweet and helpful she was trying to be while also distracting us from one of the biggest moments of our lives. Smiling, we easily settled ourselves back into the moment.

Sam and I were holding Mum's hands and stroking her arms. Her breathing was getting very slow, quietly rattling, but peaceful.

Then, it stopped.

Her stomach was still.

We looked over at Jude, giving her a look of "Maybe now?", but then Mum breathed normally again as if to say, "No, not just yet" (in retrospect, it probably was, but luckily, I don't think it buggered up the time recording). With tears slowly rolling down our cheeks, we giggled a little bit at her one last trick. She breathed another few slow, shallow, silent breaths. We told her how much we love her and would miss her. We told her what a good job she had done as our mum and how excited we were for her. All of that was said quietly, tenderly, with more than just the words. I slowly moved my head to look up and down her body, taking her full physical presence in as the four of us waited in silence.

She breathed one more time, stopping at the end of her breath out, like a subtle but definite full stop.

We looked at Jude again with more confidence, waited a few more seconds, then gave her the signal. That was it. No more breathing. 10:54 p.m. It was almost as if nothing had happened, but our mum and sister had just died, so it was a pretty big deal. No sparkly pink and silver light (from our end anyway), but it *was*, in the end, so *easy*.

Hilarious that I say it was "easy" after all we had all been through, especially Mum. But at the very end, that's how it was. We sat for a moment, tears on our cheeks. I don't recall feeling overwhelming sadness, horror, anxiety, or tiredness, even, all of which had featured in the story so strongly up until then. I didn't feel relief, but there was a sense of feeling at ease. As I said, it was almost as if nothing much had happened.

We sat with Mum for only a short while, then started getting our things together. We tidied the bench and emptied the fridge. Jude went to inform the nurses that Mum had died (and give them the exact time, whether they needed it or not), and shortly afterwards, the nurse who had almost stolen the show came in. She looked over at Mum with a look of kindness, introducing herself as Helen. Approaching Mum, she almost tripped on a chair or something, somehow. One of those stumbles that makes you think, *What did you even trip on?!* It made a loud noise in the serenity, putting her off her solemn and professional game, but also unbeknownst to her, created for her the endearing nickname "Clumsy Helen", true on both accounts of our interactions with her. She was formally part of the "cast".

Helen advised that she needed the doctor to confirm Mum's death officially, so she would knock before she came in as a heads up to whip on our masks. She said that might take a while, but we could stay as long as we wanted to, or if we wanted to go, she would make sure that Mum was in safe hands. Checking that we were all managing okay, she left, and we continued packing.

Once that was done, I cautiously went to sit with Mum. I have a phobia of "dead things", even dead fish in our tank totally freak me out. I didn't respond well to seeing relatives at funeral home viewings in the past and am still slightly haunted by the experience, and thankfully, I hadn't had a need to go through that since. Sitting with Mum for the short time after she died hadn't scared me, so I approached her with slight trepidation but felt at ease once I sat down.

Focusing on doing so distracted me from settling into the realisation that she was now dead. She was Mum, lying there, dead, rather than me comprehending what that actually meant.

I stroked her arm a little bit, which was a big deal for me to try, but I was surprised to manage that okay. I wish I could remember what I said to her. I don't think it was much other than goodbye and that I loved her. It didn't feel as weird, as sad, or as momentous as what I had obviously expected it to be. She was dead. I knew it, but it hadn't landed in me yet.

The main concern Sam and I had was having to leave her lying there all alone. We did not want her to be alone, again; that thought was more than we could bear, and at the time felt far more overwhelming than the fact that she had died. But we were ready to go, and to linger any longer would be a bit of cheek, given we had been asking her not to for so many days. Now that she had finally listened, we needed to practice what we preached.

We asked Jude if she would mind staying just a little longer, just so we could leave without seeing her by herself. Leaving her with someone who loved her and who she loved seemed a much more caring and manageable way of going about it. Of course, Jude agreed, and we turned back for one last goodbye as we walked away, piercing through the bubble, popping out into the darkness of the still night.

In her book, *Dying to be Me*, Anita Moorjani recalls her near-death experience. Her NDE (near-death experience) resulted from end-stage cancer. Subsequent to it, she was cured without medical intervention. Anita's NDE shares many similarities with other accounts I have read and those studied by specialists in that field, but it is particularly detailed, uplifting, and comforting.

While she lay dying, Anita reports that she felt completely sharp and alert. She could see, feel, and understand everything going on around her. She felt weightless, absolutely pain-free. She could be anywhere at any time. She came back telling of things that were confirmed as taking place in other rooms, let alone other countries. She could move forward and backward through time. She says she felt nothing but unconditional, pure, blissful love and total freedom. She felt as though she had transformed into love, that instead of being human, she felt as though she *was* love.

Mum's journey from her stroke to her death was a long one, so I hope, I try to believe, that Mum felt the same way for as long of her dying journey as possible. If she wasn't meant to be saved, if the result of her stroke was always going to be her death, I hope to my core that she experienced what Anita did. That time to her was irrelevant. Reality makes me believe that this wasn't the case throughout her whole ordeal. Maybe it's more likely that she slipped in and out of moments like that, especially when she was on the floor. But I feel more certain that she fell into that relief completely by the time of our afternoon send-off party, with a little sip of Guinness on her lips. I think she was totally immersed by then and felt no pain of what was to come, no "reality", only pure love, like Anita describes. All the gifts, the rattles, the secretions, they didn't seem like gifts at all at the time, they were of no concern to her. Her "easy" last few breaths were our blessing; she didn't need them; they were for us. She was already only love, not even a body, just an instrument of love.

That's all. So simple.

When her body finally stopped, she didn't even notice; it was irrelevant. That's why it felt so easy for us to comprehend, why it was so graceful, why we were able to smile. She took us with her in those few moments.

We put our masks on despite it seeming ridiculous because there was no one around, but we were back in the headspace of playing by the rules. It was the first time I had been in the front courtyard of the palliative care unit since we walked through the doors with Mum, and the first time I had been anywhere beyond the unit for days. The darkness of the last hour of that night, the silence, disturbed only by sounds of insects in the bushes, not a single (visible) soul anywhere. Wearing masks and the comprehension that Mum was dead made everything feel apocalyptic. A whole new world that I had never been to before. Surreal. After feeling so strangely safe inside my bubble of doom, I didn't feel like I belonged out there.

We drove to Sam's, masks on (as per the rules), the bright lights of the city buzzing past, and the lack of cars or people on the streets added to the feeling of being in a sci-fi movie.

We arrived at Sam's at around 1 a.m. and quickly made our way to bed. This time I was in the spare room. I felt okay, more so unnerved than upset. Little did we know, Jude hadn't understood our request to stay with Mum properly, later telling us that she sat there for over half an hour waiting for the doctor to hurry up so Mum wasn't by herself, wondering when it would be "appropriate" to leave. She said she was grateful for the extra time with just the two of them, but also wanted to get home, still; she honoured what she thought our wishes to be.

When the doctor still hadn't been, and she'd said enough goodbyes to feel at a loose end, she decided to "sneak off early". We laughed, telling her she only needed to stay for a few minutes; it was just *seeing* Mum lying there on her own while we walked away from her that we needed her help with. Her longer vigil wasn't part of the favour, but Mum appreciated it, I am sure.

AFTER

Chapter 9 — Magic

When I woke that morning, Mum being dead came to my thoughts instantly, like a quick, hard punch to the guts. The first of the months of every morning, I would wake up like that. I lay in bed listening to the noise of the household. My nieces were making normal "kids in the morning" sounds. Did they know yet? I realised Ev and the girls didn't, so I rang and spoke with Ev first, then told the girls together on loudspeaker. I can't remember the conversation clearly, but Orla tells me she can. She has an amazing memory, but this would be one life event she will hold onto for many years to come, I imagine. Ev had obviously been doing a good job with the girls because, although they were clearly sad, they handled it in a way that indicated they weren't shocked. It warmed my heart at their tender ages that they were more concerned for my well-being than they were for their own.

Once I was up, it was evident that Sam and Kel's girls knew too, so we had a cuddle, acknowledging our shared loss with a few tears. Sam and I were very keen to finally play the funeral title track, *Eagle When She Flies*, so we shooed the kids outside, made a coffee, and settled down at the kitchen table with Kel to listen. Thankfully, it was not a Super Rooster moment. Not in any way. It completely exceeded our expectations, kicking arse over anything we could have chosen ourselves. Not only because it was such a great song, *perfect* for Mum, every single line seemed to be written for her, and it was perfect for the occasion, but the fact that she chose it made it feel like she was still with us, talking to us through it.

The song was about a woman who is as powerful and magnificent as an eagle, yet also as soft and tender as a sparrow. It's about resiliency and fragility. About a woman who has experienced storms and rainbows, been everything, to everyone, a force to be reckoned with, who has always maintained a strong sense of self-pride and inner strength, despite being as delicate as a butterfly. We were speechless. What a tune! We were so happy with our decision to save hearing it for that moment, and relieved we already had such a major part of the funeral organised for us.

Cheers, Mum! As had been the case throughout the entire process, we laughed and cried, recognising and cherishing the magic of the whole situation.

The morning was very relaxed. We didn't rush to do anything, focusing primarily on notifying people like Dad and Mary that Mum had died and getting the basic beginnings of funeral planning underway, arranging to meet Jude at Mum's later that day to do so, and to "debrief".

On the drive to Mum's, we discussed what items we should see if we could find in order to store safely at Sam's while her unit was vacant, although our primary focus was on funeral preparation rather than the other jobs our booklet stipulated doing first, seeing as how we'd already created our own syllabus. We discussed paying a few weeks' extra rent so we wouldn't have to rush everything.

Upon arrival, without mention of it again and despite being well hidden for safekeeping by Mum, we had found all of the items we wanted, along with a few we hadn't thought of. It felt like she must have been listening to us and had led us by the hand to find everything, because it just eventuated as we chatted; we weren't even fully conscious that we were finding things. She was obviously able to use the magic we had no doubt she would have access to, although the speed of it took us by surprise. Within only a few minutes, we had everything on our mental list, giggling about how much fun we were having. It was exciting to be working with such a powerful angel, so despite Mum dying only hours ago, we were in a light, joyful mood. It was as though it was all laid out for us, as though she knew this was going to happen, as if she had already read the booklet.

The initial evidence of her not wasting any time learning new tricks was the first thing we found — a 2021 diary on her kitchen table, not necessarily identifiable as a diary. "For some reason", without thinking, I went straight to it and picked it up as it sat amongst a pile of papers. Entries included a shopping list on the 4th of January. The items listed on it were in the fridge and pantry, indicating she had been shopping that same day. The first few pages provided a comprehensive list of her medications, and listed her bank accounts, insurances, and other information for utilities, with password clues that would only be guessable by us. The diary showed that she had made a call to her eldest sister on the 2nd of January to wish her happy birthday for the following day, and she had also called Mary that day. Because Mary lived in Germany, their phone calls were regular rather than frequent, and contact with her sister was neither, usually just the phone call from Mum to her on her birthday. It was nice knowing she had spoken with them both so recently.

Everything was arranged in a way that made us feel like the entire process was going to be hassle-free. We knew that she was always two weeks in advance with her rent, but her records showed she had paid it recently, meaning she was four weeks in the black, so straight away we were grateful to realise that any additional money needed to help us take our time would be minimal. Everything was rolling along so easily, so despite thinking we'd focus on the funeral, we started thinking about notifying Centrelink, as per the formal curriculum, and in doing so, found that she had also recently been paid her pension. Overall, her financial situation seemed in good shape.

We had a quick look for a will, not expecting to find one, which we didn't. She would have told us if she had one. Despite hearing nightmare accounts of what can happen if you die without one, her finances and possessions were very basic, and we knew we would be in total agreement in terms of her "estate", so we weren't concerned.

By the time Jude arrived, we'd discovered Mum had more money in the bank than we realised, obviously not spending much of the inheritance she had received from her parents over 10 years earlier. We were saddened by this relatively modest amount of money; it would have been a lot to her. She could have used it to make herself more comfortable or had some fun with it. On reflection, having that little nest egg in the bank probably did help to make her feel comfortable, and going on a holiday or something of that nature on her own, when she already spent so much time alone, may not have brought her much joy anyway. It would have been enough to get her to Germany to see Mary, though. The fact that she didn't, and all of the reasons she didn't use that money, still upsets me, although I know she was delighted to be able to help Sam and me put it to good use.

We started investigating the puzzle to hopefully answer how long she had been on the floor, discovering many possibilities that were easily answered either via her diary, phone, laptop, or other evidence of the actual "crime scene" itself. Her phone history and handwritten diary entry told us she had had a phone consultation with her doctor lasting approximately five minutes, at 12:35 p.m., two days before we found her. We noted the irony of a doctor being the last person she ever spoke to, given what was looming. As Sam said, it would've been handy if it had been a fortune teller.

Presumably, she had gone back to her laptop after the appointment, saving some research information on the Whitmore Family at 1:49 p.m., which was the last trace of her. Records conveniently accessible on her CPAP showed it wasn't used that night, so we could ascertain that she had the stroke sometime after 1:49 p.m. on Monday, 4th January 2021. Sam found her at approximately 5:30 p.m. on Wednesday, January 6th, so we had the closest answer to how long she had waited that we will ever get.

We decided to call her GP on Monday to see what he could tell us (he was genuinely shocked when we did, saying she seemed perfectly fine, which goes to show how fragile life can be). The food on the bench and the lights being off when Sam found her confirmed our suspicions that she was making a late lunch, maybe an early dinner, when it happened. Going over the timeline and being there in the room made it so real, and the horror of it was so easy to visualise. We felt a strange mixture of utter depression but also relief that it was over for her, although playing detective, piecing together the clues, and solving the mystery so easily with assistance from the super sleuth herself, raised our spirits.

We moved on to locating photos for the funeral and found with them many other mementos. No surprise at all, she had kept every single card, every single crappy little crafty thing Sam and I had ever made her, every letter anyone had ever written her, every record of anything significant or otherwise that had occurred in her life, managing to do so with such careful organisation, and such a compact and creative way of storing things. So many boxes of happy memories, mixed with times of heartache and anguish. We decided to put the hard memories aside to go through another day and spent a beautiful afternoon crying, laughing, and reflecting on our lives together. It was such an incredible gift, despite or maybe because of all the times we complained that she didn't throw stuff out and gave her the impression she was silly for keeping containers that should just go in the recycling. The systematic way she kept everything using this "junk" and the absolute pleasure we were receiving from seeing our lives, and hers, laid out in front of us, was overwhelming.

Literally a lifetime of memories that would otherwise have been lost had been held so tightly by her. Kept with such care as she had moved at least 20 times since she had separated from Dad. Choosing to take them every time, along with her other changing meagre possessions, but these boxes had not been foregone and had been added to along her way with cards and gifts from her granddaughters, so the timeline was complete.

We spent hours bathed in her love through these boxes of treasures. It was as though we were back in the bubble and Mum was still there with us just as strongly, if not in a more powerful way, than when her body was physically lying there. We burnt some of her large collection of incense, had cups of tea, and ate some of the food that was so conveniently provided by her via her recent grocery shop. It was as though she knew we were coming. She hosted us so nicely, and her unit, which had once felt too small to visit for long periods comfortably, felt cosy, safe, and filled with easy love.

As the summer afternoon faded, Sam decided to go home. Jude and I continued our reminiscing session until much later into the night before finally admitting we should get some sleep, but instead of going with her as planned, I decided to stay where I was, surprised with how comfortable I was with the idea of staying alone.

Eventually, Jude went home, and it was just me (and Mum).

It had been a beautiful day, a strange mixture of the worst time and best time in my life. I was constantly feeling emotional, whether joy or sorrow, and I was comfortable with both. The depth of my emotions was exhilarating and made me so aware of all I had to be grateful for. I felt no sense of pressure whatsoever to do anything or feel any particular way. I was floating again, but this time I felt in control. Unlike the past few days, I wasn't going to sit up and find myself on the edge of the world, so far out to sea that I was too frightened or unable to get myself back to shore. This floating sensation was one of pure peace. Throughout the entire day, I had cried and laughed the saddest and happiest tears I had ever shed. I was exhausted, but also in a state of bliss. I ran a bath, recalling the few times I had spent a night at Mum's, without the kids. She would run me a bath using all her nicest salts and bubbles and encourage me to spend as long as I needed relaxing.

Lying in the bath, her bath that I now had to fill myself, without knowing she was out in the loungeroom or reading in bed, made me so lonely for her. This was how her house was without anyone in it. Her normal.

At times, I felt slightly uneasy being there on my own. No Ev, no kids. No Mum. I wasn't used to being on my own at night. It was so quiet, except for the calming sound of the waves lapping the shoreline across the road. This was how it was for her to have a bath in her quiet house. Alone.

I lay in the bath crying and missing her, talking to her, thanking her for such a wonderful day. Thanking her for running me baths, bringing me closer to Jude and Sam, and organising her things so well. For keeping all my memories for me and having fun with us, showing off her new powers. For raising me with endless love and loving my kids so much. For being so supportive of me always, and putting up with my shit, but also calling me on it so that I didn't turn into a full-blown brat. For loving me so fiercely. I cried and cried, noticing all her things, as if she were still there. Her toothbrush was sitting there, waiting. Her hairbrush was waiting. Her moisturiser, which I knew she would have used sparingly because she was raised to be frugal, a skill she had needed throughout her life. This was how it was for her to get out of the bath and be alone.

I got dressed in one of her nighties. It was too big on me and felt like a great big hug, covering me warmly, while flowing around my legs, keeping me cool.

I got into her bed and felt instantly comfortable, sinking into the mattress and falling into the pillows in a way that made me secure and relaxed, but I was still sobbing. I was so desperate for her to not have died. It was real now. She wasn't dying anymore. She was dead. I would never, ever, see, hear, or touch her again. I was here, and she wasn't, in a physical sense at least, and she would never be in this house again. She would never be at my house again. I could hardly comprehend that to be true. I was so lonely, not because I was alone there, but it felt like I was alone in the world. Not since I stood in front of the emergency department with Jude, those few days that now felt like years ago, had I registered the reality of my new life. Everything had changed. I knew that, but it was shocking, incomprehensible.

I wanted my rose quartz for comfort, so I got up and dug around in my handbag to find it, and as I did so, a silver butterfly, a broken part off a bracelet Orla had put in there weeks earlier, almost seemed to fly out at me. Not taking much notice of it and continuing to rifle through my bag, the butterfly I had "stolen" from the hospital also "flew" out, landing in my lap. I stopped.

Straight away, I registered that because I had missed the first sign, she provided another.

Smiling, I realised that two butterflies, among all the other options of crap I had in my dump site of a handbag, had flown out at me. The next thing I knew, for "some reason", without consciously moving there, I found myself standing in the kitchen on the exact spot Sam had found her. As if by instinct, I stuck the butterfly magnet from her hospital bed onto a metal storage rack on the bench and stood staring at it, dazed for a little while. It felt like the butterfly was there to protect the space. To signify the importance of this sacred spot and maybe attempt to bring the room and the energy of her while she was lying there, some peace, like a cross, at the site of a fatal car crash. I went back to my bag, found the quartz and hopped back into bed, falling asleep with surprising ease, holding the crystal in my hand.

When I woke, her death again immediately pierced my brain. I lay for a while feeling physically comfortable, appreciating the peaceful sound of the ocean slapping against the sand. A beautiful sound to wake up to. It added to the strange feeling I had had of being on holiday when we were in palliative care. What a holiday experience, eh?

I got up feeling surprisingly refreshed. I could tell it must be early. Whitewashed pale-yellow light was flickering on the walls from the gaps around the drawn blinds, on the windows that overlooked the street and ocean. I made a coffee in one of our favourite double-glazed glasses. While waiting for the jug to boil, I noticed that the butterfly I had placed above "the spot" had curled up. Its wings were no longer visible, as if the caterpillar was starting its Chrysalis stage, the transformation stage.

When I placed it there less than five hours ago, the plastic wings were bendable, sure enough, but they were rigid and open. The sun had not long ago risen, the room was dimly lit and cool, but it was as if the magnet had melted or curled from direct sun or heat, so much so that it wasn't as clearly evident that it was a butterfly anymore.

My heart skipped in a way that felt like Christmas morning as a child, waking to find that magic things had been happening while I slept. She hadn't gone far! I stood there, shocked, staring at it, before a wave of intense grief brutally crashed on me. While it was comforting to know she was still with me, this felt different to the playful ways of yesterday. Proof of her power in that moment felt sombre as I stood in the spot that she had spent some of the hardest hours of her life. I didn't cry. I was too impressed or overwhelmed by the magic to do so, but I felt heavy and quiet. I acknowledged the gift of her obviously still being able to talk to me and tell me what she was feeling.

I closed my eyes, waiting until I, too, had felt myself "through" the feeling. Once the wave calmed, I opened the blinds and windows, made myself comfy on the lounge, and enjoyed the sounds and view of the beach, and scents of salt air, incense, and coffee as I looked around, absorbing her small home; all but her spare room and the bathroom were visible from my vantage point. I hadn't realised what a large, unobstructed ocean view she had since a building across the road had been demolished sometime in the last year or so.

As I took it all in, I took *her* in. This was her. Albeit a version of her influenced by how little money she had, it was her. Lovingly decorated with her signature style. It felt homely, inviting, and warm. It was creative and interesting. I had never thought of it in that way; to the contrary, I judged her decorating style as being a bit tacky and over the top. As I sat there, realising that judgment, I couldn't believe it. How had I seen her home and therefore seen her like that? Her house, where she had lived for 10 years, far longer than any place she had lived since I was a nine-year-old girl, was lovely. From the suncatchers dangling in the windows, throwing rainbows all over the room, the way she had covered up the ugly vertical blinds with sarongs and handmade curtains, all the flourishing plants, to the considered choices of soft furnishings to tie everything together. I was sitting in the middle of such an expression of hers. Taking the time to notice her home made me feel as though I was surrounded by her. I could feel her tenderness and femininity. It was a beautiful space to be in. I wanted to stay there forever.

Her small unit had always felt uncomfortable and cramped when visiting with the kids. The lack of outside area for them to play independently always made me feel stifled, and there were too many trinkets everywhere for them to touch and potentially break. It was hard to relax and have a conversation without being interrupted by them or distracted by keeping an eye on what they were getting into. But despite how small her space was, being the grandmother she was, she had dedicated half of her spare room to the kids; they had all they could ever wish for to draw and do crafts with.

She had picked up dolls and toy cooking sets from op shops, a whole toy box of things and bought them their own bedding despite them not visiting often, let alone rarely staying overnight. Her house was hardly ever a place we all gathered as a family, and I know that made her sad and disappointed, but she understood why. Although they felt my irritation, the kids loved Mimi's place despite it. Sitting on the lounge, I saw it for the first time through their eyes. It was a fun house, a very pretty house. She had managed to cram a lot of creativity, a lot of life into it, without it looking overly busy like I had previously thought it to be. I remembered conversations where she'd asked my opinion or feedback on things like colours for cushions or throws. I had always given such flippant responses, never listened properly or worse, disagreed with an air of superiority with suggestions she made about decorating, even at times when I had the luxury of moving house by choice, or the blessing of being able to renovate one.

I sat on her small, pale pink lounge with her fluffy pink throw blanket on my lap, realising how insensitive I was. I'd never appreciated the great job she had done to turn this modest little unit into a warm and inviting home that my children loved. I was too busy seeing it from the perspective of being convenient because it provided her stability and somewhere she could afford, one less thing for me to worry about, but inconvenient because it was too small for *my* needs. I hadn't noticed how the beach seemed to be right at the doorstep, and how quiet it was despite being so close to a relatively busy road. I felt so far away from the real world as I sat overlooking the water and the street, enjoying my coffee. I realised that at times she probably felt that way too. That must have been both a blessing and a curse to her. After a nice time relaxing and reflecting, I realised I had to shift back into reality. I still hadn't updated my friends with the news of Mum's death or even told some of them that she had been in the hospital.

I called them one after the other, going through the story from the beginning to the end, and although it was a strange and heavy thing to do, I wasn't overwhelmed by doing so. I laughed with them that, at least for once, I had some actual news. It was good to have that big job ticked off the list after such a long time being "off grid".

Chapter 10 – Preparing

Sam had finally decided on the most appropriate funeral home to meet every one of his well-considered requirements, called Heartfelt Funerals. I mention the name specifically because it feels like a bit of a shame that I don't know of many people dying; I'd like to be able to send more business their way, so I figure I'll drum up a bit of interest through this book! He arranged a midday appointment to commence planning and for a viewing once we were further along the track. In all seriousness, if you live in the North Brisbane or Redcliffe area and you need someone for the job, give them a call! You won't be disappointed. Tell them Lynda sent you (or by rights, maybe you should say it was Sam).

Still wearing Mum's nightie, I spent a few hours looking through photos, enjoying the sea breeze. Strangely, I felt a real sense of peace, happiness even, like an easy Sunday morning. Eventually, I got up to get organised to go out.

The Heartfelt office was in the foyer of a small, quaint wooden church. We met Maree, who guided us along the main points we should organise and consider. We got to know her, giving her a glimpse into who Mum was and how we operate as a family. It was a totally stress-free experience, all the while I was aware that Mum's body was lying somewhere nearby. I don't think she was listening in, though. No doubt she was busy at the family reunion. A party like that would have gone on for days, so aside from taking time out to help Sam and me find her "hidden" things, I imagined she was under the shade of the family tree, busily catching up with everyone. With Maree's help, we made a list of jobs and arranged to bring back some clothes for Mum's funeral outfit. We also decided that given the two-week mask mandate, we would delay the funeral until after the proposed end date, hopeful that it would be lifted in time to not have to wear them.

It was a massive relief to be afforded that amount of time, the mask rule serving as a blessing, as we possibly wouldn't have considered that length of time otherwise. Planning that day with Maree was difficult enough with a mask on, let alone having to wear one at the funeral. We also knew it would make the experience more foreign and difficult for the kids, given that masks were such a new and strange thing. We assumed Mum would work her magic to sort it out in time.

Maree was so supportive, making everything so easy, almost "fun". Yet again, we had landed in exactly the right place, which was lucky, given the length of time Sam had dedicated to the task.

Mum had recently started treating herself to regular pedicures, something she and I had done together a few times, but something she never did just for herself. Not only because of the expense, but because she didn't care for herself in that way, despite being quite feminine and always taking care of how she presented herself. She had been very happy, and I would say proud of herself, when she reported this new intention to me. She knew she deserved it, and it gave her something to look forward to every month or so. Having had them done in time for Christmas Day, we figured her toes were still in pretty good shape. We had discussed this with Maree, deciding that aside from it being in line with a summer vibe, she should wear sandals so her turquoise polish was visible. Maree suggested that she could finish off the look by giving her a manicure, and we decided a nice shade of pink would tie in nicely with her ensemble. With everything as organised as it could be at such an early stage, we left the chapel and hit the shops to start our jobs.

Once our shopping was done, Sam dropped me back at Mum's, and I spent the remainder of the afternoon and night there again, reading through her thoughts, going through more mementos, sorting photos, and sending messages to Sam and Jude of the many funny and inspiring things I was finding. I made "to-do" lists, essentially, personalising the "what to do" booklet. Although I was relaxed and content in my own space, I spent long periods crying until my clothes were saturated, still intensified with wonder and awe at her little house that she had recently decided it was time to move on from.

For so many years before landing there, she had searched, struggled, to find stability. While certainly not perfect for many of her own reasons, let alone mine, she had finally found a home. But over the past 12 months, she had been talking about, and in some ways actively looking for, somewhere else to go. Now it worked out she had, albeit in a very different way from what we had all assumed.

She had talked about staying in the area, mainly because it was familiar and practical to do so, but at times also considered somewhere further afield. Nowhere specific. A few times, she said she'd love to live out in the country again, to be able to have a garden for veggies and flowers and maybe even get a dog. Those ideas sounded inconvenient, impractical, or silly to Sam and me. As was our way, my way in particular, I canned her ability to dream such a simplistic and happy dream, or at least, to share that dream with me, reminding her of her age and need to be close to medical help and basic amenities and refocusing her attention on it being somewhere close enough for the three of us to visit each other easily. Well, now maybe she had gotten her way. She had left her little house by the sea, which was starting to drain her for various reasons, but thankfully, still on good terms, yet I strongly sensed her still there with me, sharing the peace and freedom it had provided her. I was relieved for her and myself, I suppose, that she didn't need to worry about the stressful and practical side of where she would end up next, or perhaps that she would end up having to stay there and become more unhappy because her finances wouldn't allow her to leave.

The next day, the three of us continued our calls and planning. Kel offered to make some bookmarks to give to the funeral guests and was helping with a variety of things. Jude arrived mid-morning, just to hang, but with the lockdown being over, I decided I was ready to go home. She offered to drive me, so I didn't have to go by train. I'd considered staying another night, but really, I was ready. I had never been apart from the girls for that long, but I was so consumed in such a positive way with what I was doing, and surprisingly, was comfortable being away. Phone calls had put my mind at ease that Ev had it under control, and I knew the girls were actually capable without me and mature enough to understand that I needed that time. I was glad this hadn't happened any earlier in their lives for that, apart from other obvious reasons.

Jude suggested it would be nice to take Mum's car, and we knew Mum would be happy to shout us the fuel. The car loaded with my small bag (including my yet-to-be-necessary strapless bra), a few plants and things of Mum's I wanted, we headed towards the highway, the motorbike keyring she'd always had hanging from her rear vision mirror swaying to her Linda Ronstadt cassette tape playing on the stereo.

Another road trip, this one taking me to a new place called home. Somewhere I'd never been without Mum being alive. We phoned Jude and Mum's sister, my Aunty Chellie, on the way, chatting excitedly about all the tricks Mum had already shown us and what we were planning for her send-off party.

We arrived home and were welcomed with so much love. Everyone was very happy to have me back. The house had been turned upside down, literally, with chairs and sheets creating barriers and covers over the furniture to stop Lexi from weeing on everything. She was improving but still having occasional bouts of urinary incontinence. We laughed at how bad of a time Ev had been having to deal with that, and having to chase her to force feed her medicine twice a day, while all I was doing was relaxing down in Brisbane, watching Mum die and planning her funeral.

Arlyn had made a beautiful "Welcome Home, Mum" sign. Orla made a batch of biscuits, trying her best to mix the food dye to get my favourite shade of green, adding so much, that dye seemed to be the dominant flavour, so we had a little laugh about that too. Jude and I updated everyone, and she stayed for a short visit before heading off. As I watched her drive away in Mum's car, I remember feeling like it was the end of an era. The start of the next module, "How to successfully float between the after-death experience and reality of your day-to-day life."

***

Boxes of Mum's things lined the walls for the next few weeks while I worked unpacking them, the girls referring to things as "stolen from Mimi" when they would come across items that now belonged to us. My aunty and uncle on Dad's side, Mary, and two of Mum's university friends from all those years ago, sent flowers. That was a lovely surprise. I was so touched that people were thinking of me, but more so, honouring Mum in that way. Despite the mess and flowers, I realised how clinical my house looked in comparison to hers. Mum often gently tried to encourage me to use more colour or add things to give our home a bit more "pizzazz". I was happy being back in my own space, but missed being at Mum's because of how strongly I could feel her there, so I was glad I could add little touches of her into my home to give it some of her warmth. I started to develop my new relationship with her without really realising it because of this topic, having the first of many jokes with her that all she had to do was die to get me to listen and agree with her on things. I have become quite the obedient daughter since her death, often sharing a laugh with her about that, as she rolls her eyes, I am sure.

The unpacking and funeral preparations meant that my usual attention to housework and routine with the kids was lacking, so it was a bit of a chaotic time, but it was a magical headspace to be in, immersed in Mum via both her physical presence through her things, and through her spirit that I felt with me throughout that time. I was also in regular contact with "the gang" and therefore, still in "the bubble" to a degree.

Regularly throughout each day, we were reminding each other of the "good times" in hospital, sharing our 'in jokes' and enjoying being part of that club, while still remembering to be open, present, and connected to those who weren't founding members. Sam and Jude had opportunities individually to spend time at Mum's, and while organising and packing, they discovered that she had bits of cash stashed away, enough to cover funeral and wake expenses, let alone the money in the bank, which was already more than enough. They also uncovered a treasure trove of scribblings, enlightened and curious little messages that she had obviously recorded both in haste and in a more organised, reflected upon fashion. Written in a way that felt like she was still communicating with us "from beyond". Mental notes of her wisdom were scratched down beside shopping lists and recipes, as if the deep and the everyday were one and the same, and funny little insights like number plates of dangerous drivers that made us laugh and made it seem as though she was still speaking to us. Those things were the true valuables. I am so lucky and grateful to have so much of her handwriting and so much insight and reminders through it, of her thought processes and what was meaningful to her.

Over the next fortnight, we continued along our processing journey. Having such a luxurious amount of time before the funeral was a necessary and perfect way to commence the grieving process. Gathering stories and photos and collating all those memories and mixing them with music, family connection, summer, love, tears, and laughter without time pressures, was one of the pleasures of my lifetime.

The practical side of tying up Mum's existence was also keeping us busy. Notifying Centrelink, the real estate, insurance companies and the like, and we met with Jo, our funeral celebrant, another of Sam's meticulous searching jackpot finds, so we were well on our way to knocking Module 6.75 out of the park. Like Maree and unlike so many people in this day and age of "amazing" people, Jo was just so normal, grounded, warm, and good-humoured. She seemed genuinely interested in getting to know Mum through us and really listened to what was important to us and was able to guide us exactly where we needed to go. We enjoyed a few hours with her in Mum's loungeroom, chatting, planning, drinking tea, and eating familiar old family favourites like cheese and tomato on crackers with lots of butter, pepper, and salt.

The following week, we finalised the songs for each "scene" of the funeral, the order of service, photos for a montage, and venue and menu for the wake. We decided that the kids would decorate the top of the coffin with a selection of Mum's scarves, crystals, and trinkets that they felt best signified their Mimi. We'd made a death announcement on Facebook, and provided funeral details, confidently keeping our fingers crossed that the mask mandate would be lifted in time, and had met Clint, another member of the beautiful Heartfelt Funeral team (who would eventually be cast in the story with his own nickname). We had also been to see Mum.

I went along to the viewing with no intention of seeing Mum, fearful that it might cause me more distress than closure. I sat in the waiting room while Sam and Jude went in, and shortly after, Jude came back out and gently encouraged me to join her. I made a quick decision without overthinking it, figuring I'd just ease my way in so that I could only see a "little bit of her", and that was easier than I imagined, so I decided to just go for it. She had some bruising on part of her face, and her face was also a bit flat, sunken, or kind of "wind swept". Aside from that, she looked quite okay. Maree had done a beautiful job of dressing her in the outfit we all agreed was one of her nicest ensembles. We had chosen some small items from her treasures to go with her on her journey. A small, beaded bag filled with crystal chips (presents from the fairies she used to tell the girls), a statue of the Virgin Mary, a family tree-shaped pendant engraved with our immediate family's names (a birthday present from Sam and me a few years earlier) and a locket with a photo of Sam and me inside. These had been placed on her chest and in her hands, and her fingernails were nicely painted with the pink polish.

It was a very surreal experience; inspecting her almost. Maree had done her hair nicely, and she was dressed in her floaty summer outfit with a matching lightweight scarf that looked good. But she was dead. Yellow hands and a weird, flat face dead. I was relieved not to feel scared of her, and the experience wasn't negative. I think now that it was a good thing to do for the grieving process overall, but at the time, it felt a bit voyeuristic, to me at least. I talked myself into touching her briefly, but unlike Jude, I wasn't keen on that either. So, not long after saying "Hello Mum", I said goodbye to her again, in person, for the last time ever.

Rolling into the funeral week, booked for a Friday afternoon (the best day for a funeral in our humble opinion, Module 6.75 was probably the unit we got a High Distinction for) with everything in order aside from my speech, Ev and I decided to take the girls camping for a few nights up in the Hinterland not far from where we live. I felt so blessed to be able to combine having a family holiday in nature at my favourite time of year, while freshly grieving my mother's death and processing all that led up to it. It felt like everything was aligning, while simultaneously, the worst time of my life was unfolding. We regularly joked, but with a sense of truth, that Mum died at such a convenient time for so many reasons. We'd enjoyed a beautiful Christmas together, and there was still almost 12 months until the next one, so Christmas never really needed to be a shattered memory or a hard time of year. She'd made it into the new year, which seemed to be providing her with a feeling of hope and promise of a fresh start. We were afforded the luxury of having more time than usual to plan the funeral, and even with that extra week, we still had time to have the service before the kids were due back for the start of the school year. Little things did not go unnoticed by me, like not having the pressure of shopping for school supplies. Uncharacteristically, without knowing what was to come, I had ordered everything online a few hours before I rang Sam to tell him that Mum wasn't answering my calls.

I had been experiencing high anxiety about Orla starting high school for about 12 months in the lead-up, and with the first day only weeks away, she was also feeling very hesitant. Considering this, although I wasn't necessarily looking forward to it, I felt a surprising sense of calm. The shift in focus from this impending milestone to planning the funeral was, in many ways, a relief. It wasn't lost on me that the timing was good, and that feeling relief was, at the very least, a bit weird. But if those two worlds collided closer, I am sure I would not have had the strength to handle either of the situations with such resilience. My kids always come first, so I was grateful that I could give Mum the time and focus she deserved without the overlap of worrying about Orla, or my anxiety about that overshadowing my grief in any way. Perhaps it was also Mum using her magic to help settle me.

The timing of the summer holidays also meant that I was able to spend a beautiful time in the lead-up to both life events, relaxing with my husband and kids in our relatively new campervan, immersed in peaceful love and sunshine as my heart ached and my tears fell. Aside from timing aspects, I was also aware that as an adult, organising the funeral of a parent was something I was very lucky to experience, rather than the other way around. As can often be the case in life, something good was crossing paths with something bad. Considering how bad the something bad was, everything else was falling into place, so gratitude was so easy to access despite it.

Chapter 11 — Honouring

Three days before the funeral, the only lingering job was writing my speech. I felt such apprehension that nothing would come or make sense, and that the process would be lost in making it sound right, rather than being able to express the depth of my feelings and why Mum meant so much to me. Sam was working on the eulogy, and all five granddaughters had written something that our celebrant, Jo, would read on their behalf, and although everything else for the service was in order, I was becoming increasingly nervous about time ticking away and the self-driven pressure to write something meaningful, so I allocated some quiet time to get started.

To my surprise, without stopping (aside from blowing my nose and washing my face so I could see the keyboard through my tears), in a very short time, I had poured out a letter to Mum that conveyed all that I wanted it to. It was such a cathartic experience. I sensed her sitting beside me as I typed. With a few tweaks and everything else finalised by the end of that day, I had a shower and started to wind down. The days were so heavy and busy, and I had been up late every night since Mum died, so I planned an early night.

Sam called as I was getting into bed, quickly asking if I had recently spoken to Dad. When I reported I hadn't, he told me Dad was in the hospital. He had had a heart attack sometime that day. A heart attack! Sometime today! I was in such a spin I almost found it funny. Dad had a history of heart issues, having had some minor surgeries around 15 years ago, but to my knowledge, he hadn't had much of significance happen in that department for quite some time.

Instantly, I got up to get ready to get there quickly before he died, before Sam insisted it wasn't necessary, assuring me that he was likely going to be fine. The only reason he even knew it had happened was because he'd called Dad to clarify some information for his eulogy and Dad had casually mentioned afterwards that he'd had to call an ambulance earlier that day. He wasn't planning to tell us, just yet at least, but felt obligated to, seeing how Sam had called. He'd probably been stressing about worrying us, more than the fact that he was unwell. Although it wasn't necessary, or the right way to go about it, I appreciated the consideration and understood how anxious the timing of this would have felt for him, but I hated the thought that he was worried he was burdening us.

I was in a state of shock. He had taken my girls to Aussie World the day before to give me space to write my speech, the first outing of its kind for just the three of them. Maybe that had been too much for him? Or was it Mum dying that had contributed? Mum was dead! Dad had had a heart attack! Far out! What the fuck?

Convinced by Sam, it didn't seem to be a life-threatening problem at this stage, at least. I sat gathering my thoughts, crying and feeling absolutely gut-wrenchingly sad that he might not be well enough to make it to the funeral. It hadn't occurred to me how important it was to me that he be there to support us, and to show him what a good job his three kids had done (the hospital staff kept referring to Mum as Jude's mother, so by default, Dad had since claimed her as his daughter too, becoming yet another of those "family jokes"). I also wanted to share with him how much love we had for Mum. For him to witness how important she was to us, to prove that to him, perhaps?

I wanted him there because he is my dad, my now only parent, and I didn't want to feel like I was alone in that area, because I wasn't. He should be there. Unlike my feelings and reaction to him at the hospital, he very much belonged in that space. I was in such a state of shock over the fragility of life that I had a clarity of awareness of how different it is to experience that frailty, rather than it just being something my stress-head little brain had so often considered as an abstract concept. I was devastated imagining him having had a heart attack, made worse by the fact that I didn't even know and that he was on his own without support from Sam and me, because he very well may have died too. With those thoughts racing, I pulled myself together and called him. He sounded distressed about bothering me, which made me sadder, but at least he was okay. After confirming for sure that he was stable and arranging to visit tomorrow, I hung up and had another cry, asking Mum to look after him and, if possible, get him to the funeral. Then, with surprising ease, I fell asleep.

I spent a few hours with Dad the next day. He was agitated by the delay in being seen for tests, the lack of information, let alone updates, and was hungry because he was left nil by mouth for a long period because of these supposed impending tests. He was stressed and given the reason for his admission, so was I, so I sat with him for as long as I could to distract him from his hunger and boredom.

I've always had this strange thing with my dad that I hate knowing that he's upset or struggling; in a different, more intense way than how Mum feeling like that ever made me feel. Comparatively, very much so, I took her more for granted.

In contrast to how I responded to Mum, I put Dad's feelings ahead of my own. I want to fix things for him, to never be a bother or a burden to him. I try to ensure that I am never the cause of him feeling uncomfortable or unhappy. It stems from my need to get his approval (that's what Mum used to say, and she was right) in a way that I never had with her. I treated her badly at times because I felt in my core the unconditional aspect of her love. Not that I in any way have ever doubted Dad's love, but I wasn't ever guarded with her like that, and that meant that I didn't try as hard with or for her, and in actual fact, on some level at times, didn't try at all.

Dad being as upset as he was about Mum dying and now being in hospital, made things feel like I had somehow accidentally floated into another bubble; a "bad things keep happening" kind of bubble where the outside world keeps moving along, but just as one bubble almost bursts, it joins onto another as they can do. It felt like I was watching the "real world", where I used to live, where nothing much happens, roll along outside, from inside the oily lens of this "double bubble". Mum's death was hard enough, but I hadn't had a chance to catch my breath before attaching to this new bubble.

The girls found out that Dad was in hospital by accident. I felt that even though Dad should have told Sam and me, his grown-up kids, it seemed he would be okay, so the rawness of what they were already dealing with meant they didn't need that added to. That was the plan, at least until Orla overheard me discussing it with a friend when I didn't realise she was in earshot, piping up with a "What? Papa's in hospital!?"

Subsequently, I explained what had happened to both girls, and they trusted my assurance that he was alright. The following day (why did we ever doubt Mum's powers), Dad was well enough to be discharged with follow-up tests scheduled. He was a bit frail, but stable, and his brother, Garry, came up from northern New South Wales that afternoon to be with him. Apparently, he had already planned to come to the funeral, which surprised but pleased me. Mum's help with getting Dad out in time would've definitely been to provide us with his support, but no doubt, she would've also wanted him there for her own reasons and knowing her as I do, she probably felt that *he* needed to be there for his own karmic reasons too.

Sam, Kel, and the girls arrived at our place the evening before the funeral so we could practice our speeches together and ensure everything was organised. The girls hadn't seen each other since the day in palliative care and needed to get together to each choose one of Mum's scarves they wanted to wear, which trinkets to put on the coffin, and to get crafty and "bedazzle" a large timber frame to display the Mimi version photo of Mum to sit by her coffin opposite a black and white one of her in her younger years. Kel's bookmarks were beautiful, a little rose quartz hanging from each one. We had a collection of handkerchiefs once belonging to Nanna and Dadda that Jude had never known what to do with, so we decided the kids could hand them out as people arrived. A welcome gift, or "souvenir" of sorts, that, whilst possibly practical, was also a nod to our dadda, who was known for his hankies.

Again, as if there should have been any doubt in Mum's ability, the mask mandate was lifted at 12 a.m. that day, and the restricted numbers for gatherings didn't impact our plans. A last-minute change of start time to allow for a COVID clean of the venue felt like a major issue at the time, but it didn't pose an issue for anyone, and we were off and running, eventually, once Jude finally arrived late, after stopping on the side of the road on her drive there, for a "grief meltdown".

The funeral really honoured Mum, perfectly depicting her roles as woman, mother, mother-in-law, daughter, sister, friend, and grandmother. It was all we planned and hoped it would be. She was loved, and the hole left by her absence was evident. But it was also joyful. I had a strange reaction when people started arriving, having to pull myself back from greeting them as if it were my wedding or a special birthday celebration. I probably seemed way too excited, but I was so happy to see everyone show up for her. Jo and Maree facilitated everything seamlessly with professionalism and warmth. The support they provided the whole time was the sole reason we had been able to experience the entire process with such composure and recognise it as such a gift (a quiet nod there to Sam and his "pointless, pedantic" research). Our five girls did a lovely job with the frame and coffin, and handed out the hankies, cards, and bookmarks to the guests.

Jo read the girls' heartfelt tributes, making everyone cry; Sam and I got through our speeches without too much choking, and Jude read the *Hold Your Heart in my Heart* poem beautifully. The photo montage of Mum's life and the soundtrack that accompanied it were heartbreaking and uplifting. Dad being there was such a relief; I needed his support, but more so, I wanted to share this intimate experience with him. I so deeply appreciated for us, and for Mum, that people I would not have expected would even really register her death, travelled distances to be there. The surprise addition of these people truly moved me.

We gathered afterwards at an airy seaside restaurant not far from Mum's place, where on a few occasions we had gone to lunch together. The same place I was going to suggest we go for lunch when I was trying to call her all those weeks ago, before the world had warped.

Organising the wake was a pleasure for Sam and me. We love hosting "a good do", and to honour our mum, it was deeply important to us that we created the right atmosphere. She would have been so pleased that her money was used to shout everyone something to eat. She was always so generous with the little money she had, regularly doing things like that on a much smaller scale. We made a playlist, aptly titled by Sam: "Wake Me Up Before Mum Goes Go", and songs in the tune of Mum played, as we enjoyed the gorgeous summer weather with a lovely "Friday after work drinks" kind of vibe.

Long after the wake was officially over, after a traditionally long McCabe goodbye, we headed home. I cried, to put it more accurately, I *howled* all the way there as I listened to songs that would continue to be my soundtrack for the next few months. That trip home really upset Orla. She was so sad, and my sorrow filling the car didn't help, yet she sat quietly in the backseat, maturely understanding that I needed to process the day in that way. Sam, Kel, Jude, and the girls stayed again that night, and we spent the evening video calling family in Western Australia who had tuned in to the funeral via Zoom, filling them in on the events of the afterparty and reminiscing about Mum and other dead people in our family.

Mum was no longer physically on the planet. She had officially been "burnt", as Arlyn had put it after the funeral, as we watched the hearse drive away from the guard of honour. One huge part of the process was complete. More to add to the memories and the folklore of Mum's life and death. We spent the weekend relaxing and swimming in the pool with almost a Christmas Day vibe, making plans to meet at Mum's the following weekend to pack her things and finalise her lease. The practical focus was now on finalising Mum's affairs, so onwards to Module 7.01: "Death admin" we went.

The issue of her not having a will didn't pose an issue aside from creating additional paperwork. The positive side of having no significant savings or assets, I guess, is that if you die without a will, it doesn't cause any major hassles. All in all, everything ran easily. Repeating over and over to strangers who, in the nicest possible way, didn't care, was an emotionally taxing thing to do, yet I often felt removed or distant from hearing myself saying that Mum had died.

Mum was delivered to us the week after the funeral. The beautiful Clint from Heartfelt went above and beyond our expectations by delivering her to my home, saving Sam or me the trip. Given all that we had on our plates, it was so generous of him to do so. Some unexpected work commitments delayed her arrival (I assume that's pretty common in his industry), so instead of dropping her off as planned, Clint had to reschedule for the following morning on his way to work. This meant she would be spending the night at his house. To ease any concerns he thought I might have about that (not that I did), he assured me he would take good care of her, joking that they would have a great time together. Like the leprechaun, Mum would have really liked Clint. Sam, Jude and I still have a laugh about him being the very last friend she ever made, her "sleepover" at his place earning him the nickname "Mum's mate, Clint".

Chapter 12 — Growth

In the weeks that followed, aside from unpacking her possessions, sorting through what to "steal" and what to get rid of, the emotional processing required to clear out her unit and sell her little green car were the two most intense aspects of the "death admin" module. When Sam advised the real estate agent of Mum's death, briefly explaining what had happened, the agent referred to it as a "blessing" that Mum died because "at least she wasn't a veggie". We, of course, found this rather abrupt, not to mention politically incorrect in this day and age, but rather than feel insulted, it gave us a good laugh that someone could be so blatantly insensitive, despite the fact that, in essence, it was true. We took Mum along (in her ashes 'era'), for one last weekend at home. Orla was a bit disturbed by this; it seemed a bit macabre to her. She was only beginning to learn about the wacky ways her family deal with death, as was Arlyn, however she seemed to align pretty quickly and happily posed for photos "with Mum", comfortably perched beside her in the car as we drove to drop the girls at Ev's parents, before heading to Mum's to start the "packing up possessions" module.

Sorting through Mum's things and throwing so much away was gut-wrenching. Sam, Kel, Jude, and Ev did trips to Vinnies, to the tip, and to drop things off at Jude's, while I stayed back to keep sorting and packing. On one of these occasions, I became totally overwhelmed with the concept of what we were doing. Sitting on the floor in her empty bedroom, I could smell the perfume I realised then I had barely taken notice that she sometimes wore. I sobbed. My whole body ached for her. I couldn't hold myself upright. I lay on the floor pleading for her not to be dead, begging her to know how sorry I was that I had not loved her how I did now, how she always deserved me to, thanking her for everything she had given me. I'd been loved by the best. I couldn't imagine how I would survive. No one else seemed to matter, and there was no way to fix this. I was alone, and always would be.

Standing in her echoing, vacant kitchen that Sunday afternoon (empty aside from a funeral booklet and bookmark that we left on the bench because it didn't feel right to leave without some acknowledgment of her having been there), after two long, noisy, bustling days, and driving away knowing we would never ever come back, was a gut-wrenching pain that still brings tears to my eyes even in recalling it.

***

Next on my long to-do list was selling her car. Not being a car lover, I was strangely very protective of it and found the process surprisingly confronting. I was determined that it should go to someone I deemed suitable, rather than just the highest price. Helped through the process by Dad and some good friends, I finally settled on a lovely couple who travelled down on the train all the way from North Queensland to collect it. Clearly, that effort, aside from that, they also seemed like lovely, down-to-earth people, made them worthy. The lady's name was Linda Kelly, so if that wasn't another sign, I don't know what is.

During the period of the core "death admin" module, the gravity of Mum's physical absence was so strong throughout the prerequisite "subjects" — "How to bring yourself to throw your mum's brush (with her hair in it), or her toothbrush away", for example.

Only a few weeks after her death, the first day of the new school year fell on my 44th birthday, so quickly added to those subjects was "Surviving the first birthday you've ever had in your life without your mum", as well as

"Sending your oldest child off to high school without your mum's support", and "Not being able to send a first day of school photo to your mum because she is dead" (I sent a few to her phone anyway, so I kind of cheated in that class), none of which were much fun.

We continued to be kept busy with so many other subjects within many other modules, fighting to find a space in the reality of my new life as it slowly kept sinking in that I would never see her again. I think it will be that way, if not forever, for a very long time — as though it is always slowly sinking in. I know she's dead, and I can't ever forget it; not a day goes by that it doesn't smack me in the face. But I also can't believe it; it's so hard to comprehend. It's a combination of a constant realisation and recurring, yet surprise attack, thought, running in parallel. A nagging yet shocking awareness that I now walk my whole life ahead without her, resulting in times where the depth of my appreciation for life is impacted because I just want to die to be able to see her. In those early days, throughout every single hour and still now, every single day, *yearning* to be able to tell her face-to-face how different I feel without her, and how much I love her. To ask her advice or her opinion, ask more questions about her. To lie next to her, hugging her, crying to her about how much I missed her every single day she was gone.

With the affairs all sorted, life was rolling along as it does, and every day and night, I deeply grieved. I would catch myself realising that, for some other person, some other family out there, this was their last moments together. I would imagine different scenarios in which, at that very moment, people were dying. Someone *just* took their last breath. All across the world, people were watching that happen to their loved ones, in whatever context it was being experienced, and their lives were about to drastically change forever. Sometimes I imagined that person to be a young child and the dying person their mother, and my heart would bleed. My, at times, pessimistic nature was finally of some good use, because a lot of my imagined scenarios were horrendous, so the reality of my situation verified how much I have to be grateful for.

Mum taught me the skill of harnessing perception. While never being dismissive, she encouraged me to focus on all that I have, rather than what I don't. To assess my wider circumstances as a tool to access gratitude. So, I realise that even Mum was lucky. Aged 67, she was far too young to die, and the drawn-out nature, particularly the time she spent alone and having to live the rest of my life without her, holds intense pain for me. But the uncomfortable or honest reality is that I know Mum is now at peace.

I mean, her life here was fine. She was in relatively good health compared to a lot of people. She didn't live a life dominated completely by physical pain. She had a family that loved her, even if she wasn't always understood. Her financial situation was very limiting, but she could pay her bills and buy little extras often enough. She lived a quiet, and she would say, very lonely and boring existence at times. She was very philosophical, very quiet-natured, but her solitary lifestyle meant that, at times, those beautiful qualities could be amplified in ways that didn't always serve her well.

I take ownership of some of that. I didn't spend as much time with her as I could have, should have, or would now if I could. I left her alone more than was necessary, and because she was by herself, she sometimes drowned in her thoughts. We discussed her tendency to do so many times. Because she lived like that, I know that she is very much at peace with this next chapter of her existence. She doesn't feel her pain or sadness now. I am aware that I couldn't have "fixed" things completely, and I don't take responsibility for the direction her life took or her responses or choices, but I could have helped her more. I wish I had eased some of that pain rather than death solving it for her, because I could have. That I know to be true.

Not that it was her intention to die, but I can feel her at peace now, free of her heavy load, and I believe she is in a much better place, so I am happy for her. I'm perhaps strangely very happy for her. In many ways, I feel that she wasn't really meant for this world. Possibly, I feel *her* relief?

A burden I used to carry has lifted as well. I don't have to worry about things like her having a car crash (she claimed to be a great driver, although as her occasional passenger, now that she's dead and I can't upset her by saying so, I in no way support that theory), or (ironically) her having a fall, or finding somewhere she could afford to live, or even feeling sad that she was so lonely. When I first began feeling that relief, I felt so callous, so disrespectful. The idea that she can possibly read my mind is something that still troubles me, so when those thoughts first started, the internal dialogue that would go on to make sure she knew that didn't mean I was glad she was dead was quite intense. I was really distressed that she might misunderstand me; however, I figured if she had mind-reading powers, surely that also meant she would understand all the nuances. She knew me to the core anyway and certainly knew I could be very blunt. Still, it was unnerving, so I'd quickly try to stop and explain.

During that time, I came across a story in one of the many books I read on death, written by a mother who felt a similar sense of relief about her child dying. She loved her daughter deeply, cared for her selflessly, but she acknowledged in confessional style that she had also drained her on a soul level, worried her endlessly. Throughout her life journey, her daughter never seemed to fit. She had done all she could, to no avail, to fix or to help her embrace that. I really related to what she felt, and maybe because Mum's aren't generally allowed to admit that sort of thing, it made me, as a daughter, feel less guilty.

Her story didn't have anything to do with a lack of love; to the contrary, as I see it. She loved her so much that she knew she was better than this world, and was therefore happy for her, despite being devastated to have lost the physical version of her beloved child. It helped me feel less alone and less heartless about my similar thoughts.

I have since come to realise, in part through talking it over with Mum during our regular chats, that none of my negative or guilty thoughts or feelings will ever diminish my love. The immense love runs parallel, and death offers a broad spectrum of ways to process things. Maybe I'm justifying it, but it's also about putting my own pain and my missing her aside and allowing the feeling of happiness I eventually began to feel for her to dominate. I truly believe that where she is now suits her style much better. From what I've read and believe, she is in a beautiful place. She is free, heard, and finally understood. So, although I'm surprised to feel it so early in my forever-ongoing grief, my acceptance of her death, even if it is attached to that uncomfortable relief, comes from how much love I have for her, not that I have just moved on or in any way because I am pleased that she is dead. It's happiness for *her*. It's also a solid expression of how well she raised us. To be able to stand on our own two feet. To know when to ask for help, but not be completely reliant on others, even her. She protected us but didn't shelter us from experiencing life's hard times, so we had room to build resilience. There's no doubt that is coming into play now in my grieving process. She did her job well.

Despite that, I'd so love to be able to check for sure that she is, in fact, okay with me being okay. Let's face it, I'd love to be able to talk to her about absolutely anything. We talked about everything, for hours, and I'm not the same person without those long talks that provided me with just a sounding board, let alone advice. It's so strange to not be able to discuss her death and its aftermath. Such a big deal event in our lives, we should be hashing it out, sharing our perspectives on what was going on. I should be getting her advice, praise, and even being "chipped" on what I could have done or be doing differently. Although we had time to be with her and begin to process it, the sudden nature and circumstances of her death meant that we couldn't discuss how she felt about the fact that she was dying.

There were times we would talk about death, but it was obviously from an abstract and broad perspective. We'd talk about it in jest or as it related to our grief responses. I know she believed in a version of heaven, but that too wasn't a topic we explored as much as I wish we had. Given the breadth of topics our crapping-on sessions would cover, it's weird that we didn't talk about death in a more meaningful way, pertaining to our own deaths, and I'm sad that we didn't, especially with my newfound appreciation and, in some ways, fascination with death and the afterlife.

I assume that if we had some warning that death was

more imminent, or the ability to talk about it while it was happening, I'd have more closure or be grieving differently. I'd love to know her thoughts, hopes, and fears about the end of her life. I don't fixate on that; I can't really complain, but I do wish we had that opportunity.

I talk to her every day, and I love our witty little chats. She will always be my main confidant, but already and more so as I get older, I will have to guess what she would say because as my life rolls on, there are so many topics that weren't covered. That often makes me feel lost. As I typed the word "guess" there, Mum insisted I edit to say "I'll just have to listen harder" to her ongoing guidance.

Anyway, Mum, true, but on with *my* story...

Perhaps the lack of all-day-long phone conversations, regular text updates, or just subconsciously knowing she was there, is why she is on my mind so often now, drastically more so than when she was alive. Although I am coping, I am *always* thinking about her. Every day. Every. Single. Day. Multiple times throughout the day.

Perhaps that is why I am coping? I console myself about any guilty thoughts by thinking that if she can read my mind, at least she surely knows she is never forgotten. I've often wondered if it is actually her, making me think of her. If that's true, she's loving that ability and is clearly revelling in the limelight! I second-guess a lot of my thoughts now, wondering if solutions I come up with are mine, or if that's her, chatting, helping, giving me the answers? That's comforting, but also annoying sometimes! Can I really give myself credit for anything I work out now? I suppose, when I feel I am doing well and keeping my life on track, I owe that to her, regardless of what she might be putting in my head, because she taught me how. I suppose she deserves part of the credit either way. (I am sharing a little laugh with her now as I write that!)

Despite justifying my remorseful, deep, dark thoughts, or even when I own my guilt about having them, there is a burden that will never lift. With all this growth and expanded insight, how I wish we could enjoy this version of our relationship, this version of me, face-to-face. We were close, but what we have now is even deeper, and there's no bullshit in our mother-daughter dynamic. It's just us being us, but not getting in the way of each other.

My guess, though, is that it may never have eventuated any other way. So, as well as some relief, I also admit in a way that is tightly entwined with deeply missing her, to being grateful for the growth her death has facilitated in me. I recognise I was so far from who I am now. If she were still here, I'd probably still be a pain in the arse, evolving, but still slowly growing up. My preference would be that she were alive, but she isn't. Sometimes, I wish that she died to get me to where I am, but resurrected so we can start again with my newfound maturity, although I think I would feel bad taking her death away from her now that she has that gift. I would understand if she didn't want to come back, but if she did, I still wouldn't hold the power to make her life totally fulfilling, nor am I responsible for doing so. She really did give it a red-hot go, many times, but it would still be up to her to expand her circumstances. Even if I did step up more, it would be likely that she would still be fairly lonely. Her dying has solved that for her and switched things; now it's me doing the longing. Missing her is now *my* burden. As a daughter who has lost her mother, as opposed to a mother who has lost her daughter, not only can I handle that, but with our particular dynamic, I owe it to her.

I hated the guilt, although I did very little to fix it. I hated the sadness I felt seeing her standing alone on the street as I drove away from an infrequent visit, waving me goodbye till my car was out of sight. Her death has been the catalyst for so much personal growth. I do put her first more now, but I will never stop desperately wishing for my own selfish needs, that I could physically share this new me with her and witness her enjoying us.

I'm in a new stage of my parenting now. I have so much to share and ask her about. Missing her as I raise teenagers is such a punch in the gut. I relate to her so much more because I can remember our relationship very well from when I was a teenager. Every day I really need her advice, comfort and help, as I often feel like I am living on a knife's edge. She deserves her afterlife, but I still need her here. I can tell her I love her as much as I like, but her death robs me of the opportunity to be able to give her the affection she craved, not judge her so harshly, listen to her with more of an open heart, and learn from her more. She needed that, but now I *need* that. Telling her I love her now, finally growing up into the woman she knew I could be, will never balance not doing those things, especially when, unlike so many people, for so many years, I was gifted that opportunity.

Certainly, for my sake, but more so hers, I feel desperately sad that, for whatever reason, I never allowed myself to fully dive into the depths of the relationship I knew I could trust while she was here. I didn't tell her enough how proud of her I was, or how lucky I knew I was to be loved by her so genuinely, or even do something as simple as touch her more often.

Sometimes, she would say I was punishing her for leaving me when I was a child. Maybe unconsciously, I was. We used to have massive fights and scream at each other. Our points of view were often at total opposite ends of the spectrum in those intense clashes, and I felt she didn't take her share of responsibility for the reasons we were fighting. Despite our, at times, tumultuous relationship, I knew she was immensely proud of me. She always supported my life choices and encouraged me to be myself. She knew me deeply and, despite that, loved *all of me*. She was open with me about my flaws rather than raising me with the impression that I was perfect, but she made it very clear that I was capable. She supported my development through encouraging self-reflection. As it turns out, my grief is completely informed by that confidence in my ability and lessons on introspection.

The balanced serving of awe she felt about things I may never have recognised otherwise in myself as special, and honesty about parts of my personality she found difficult, was a true and beautiful gift. I learnt I was a real, multi-dimensional person, worthy of love despite, and because of, my imperfections. Through her always loving eyes, I learnt to tolerate imperfections in others, have empathy and be humble. Her sometimes-said, sometimes-unsaid feedback allowed me to see my reflection very clearly and instilled self-worth and self-reflection in me in equal measures. It was one of the reasons she was proud of herself as a mother. She was open about acknowledging that. She didn't think she was perfect, but it was a job she rarely did on autopilot.

She really was a great mum, but man, she used to annoy me when I was growing up! She was always trying to teach me stuff, telling me what to do when, in my opinion, with all my years of wisdom, I was perfectly capable without her breathing down my neck, trying to help me all the time.

"Helping me all the time". What a drag to have a Mum like that, eh?

My girls would enthusiastically confirm that I have a tendency to do the same to them. Now I get it! I do control things too much, out of love, yes, but it doesn't serve any of us well to do. I am aware that they are supposed to be know-it-alls at their ages; they have it in their genetics as well, perhaps, but as mothers, she and I are freakishly similar, and she pops out of my mouth on an alarmingly frequent basis!

We are motivated by the same end goals. Like me, she was dedicated (desperate in some ways) to ensuring I was happy, safe, well-liked, so that my life would be, at the least, a good one. "Telling me how to do things all the time" came from wanting to be confident that I could manage my own life, rather than my impression that it was because she thought I couldn't, as I saw it back then. She was raising me for God's sake. *Now* I realise. I couldn't do any of that without her help. I probably wouldn't be any of the things that I proudly now am, without her "nagging" (otherwise known as guidance and sacrifices).

Hopefully, like her, I am demonstrating to my girls that I always stay true to myself, so they do the same for themselves. Mum always, *always*, treated herself with respect and kindness. Once I was an adult, she told me that I was the driving force in her decision to leave Dad. It wasn't a relationship she wanted either Sam or I to emulate. She always made it very clear to me, and to everyone, that she wasn't someone who could be shit on.

She spoke up if she felt she was being taken for granted. She modelled self-dignity and self-care to me always. That spoke louder than any words she probably also said about such things. So many gifts, yet as a know-it-all teenager (and often as a dumb-arse adult), I thought she should just be "quieter" and not make such a fuss about me railroading her. It seemed that other mums seemed to put up with whatever crap their children dished out, or at least didn't carry on as much about it. I wished she would just deal with my high, and sometimes disrespectful, expectations of her. I thought she was such a control freak.

The first six months of Orla's life were an intense struggle for me. First time mothering an emotionally sensitive but also colicky baby (probably a physical demonstration of that disposition), I directed everyone, including Mum, away, insisting on navigating the exhausting, dark tunnel of early motherhood on my own. I had no doubt during that time that she wanted to be there and would do anything for me at any time, but I pushed her out.

Although I have only realised it, in my post-her-death reflections, to her credit, she allowed me the space to go about it the way I thought I needed to. She stepped to the side, not a hint of control freak. She knew me so well, knew that independence was such a driving force within me and, I see now, trusted me on my path. She suffered watching me suffer, yet she pushed that pain and her desperate yearning to guide me to the back of the queue of importance. She had had the same hard experience with newborn me. She related, so she knew how to help, but she let me do it my way. It must have been so stressful watching me take that harder, lonelier option, stepping in when she was "allowed" to, but she didn't make it about her in any way.

It was my life, my choice, my mothering journey that I needed to start on my own terms. She offered me her hand, but didn't jump up and down when I didn't take it. She just kept her eyes on me from afar and waited patiently.

I am the control freak. It was all about me. I didn't take her needs as a mother or a new grandmother into account at all. My children are still kids, but I can't imagine having the capacity to be that open, to not insist on at least adding my own agenda in that scenario. I don't know that I could put my anxiety, knowledge, and life skills to the side and give them that level of freedom to sink, while maintaining confidence that eventually they would swim. That takes a type of guts, belief, and trust in my parenting and in my kids, that I don't yet have. She just said to me now, as I write, sit, and ponder this: *You'll get there. You are, in fact, much more of a control freak than I ever was, but you'll get there.*

I am already aware of what a massive difference it is to be a mother without being mothered. I have Ev, but she is the one and only person I could relate to and relay things to in a way that would fully understand where I'm coming from, not only *as* a mother, but also as *my* mother. I am grateful for the years I had her after I became a parent, but I feel totally alone; my mothering now feels very, very lonely without her physically here.

We still chat, but I miss being able to talk about how they're changing and tell her things they did and said, or laugh about how much like me they are becoming and in doing so, admitting how that's making me aware of how much like her I am becoming. I imagine her shock if she were to walk into the room and see how different they look, particularly Arlyn. She has physically changed so much. She would be so amazed by them; she always was, though. Perhaps even more so, I desperately miss her talking about *me* and having that feedback help inform how I parent.

I remember when Orla and Arlyn reached the ages that Sam and I were when Mum and Dad separated. The girls happen to be the same age gap as he and I, so it really highlighted how much children of those ages still need their mummy. Reflecting on that time whilst witnessing her granddaughter's innocence was heartbreaking for her. Now, the girls are the ages Sam and I were when we moved back to live with Mum. I know this milestone would be extremely significant to her. I have very clear memories of how we related back then, so we would be discussing so much about that in relation to both girls, but because Orla is the age I was, that dynamic would be so useful to compare and share our perspectives. Not only would that be creating a learning opportunity for me, but also, perhaps, a space of healing for both of us.

The irony of starting motherhood as I did, blocking her so much, and then her dying just as I was approaching mothering through the teen years makes it even more painful, and more evident how much I need her. I believe that even if we continued to clash, I would have eventually surrendered to her safe love and, through this chapter of my mothering journey, would have become more receptive to her insights and generous toward her. This stage of motherhood makes me wonder if she did actually need to die for me to grow up after all? Maybe this time in my life would have facilitated that without me having to endure this loss. Maybe. Then again, maybe I'm giving myself too much credit.

So many stories from my own pre-teen and teen years we could share, though, and in doing so, relate to each other both as women and as mothers more so than we had. I reflect on those years with Mum as time unfolds with my girls, and it makes me ache for her.

Here again, the curse of losing her when I did is also something to find gratitude in. I cannot comprehend how extremely exhausting and impossible it would feel to have lost her when my babies were babies. My perspective is *certainly* informed by having had the space to be with Mum and grieve her the way that I did initially, which was definitely due to my girls being the ages they were. If it had been when the girls were a lot younger, without doubt, I would have been overwhelmed to the point of breakdown.

In some ways, having to get up and care for them, their innocence and softness would provide solace, but being able to grieve freely without the daily slog of the physical and emotional requirements of mothering babies and young children, or the constant realisation that my children would never experience even being held by my mother, let alone, develop a relationship with her and her with them, is yet another source of gratitude.

The concept of those alternative shifts everything. My heart weeps with the thought of never witnessing the love and joy they brought to each other's lives, that I may not have had the luxury of time that allowed me to see her in her grandmother role; that *she* may have missed out on that experience. Sharing the years we were mothers together changes the whole game. Those years gave me the opportunity to develop our relationship to the point that, despite feeling regret about many things, I am not broken by it, but for any of us who have our mothers die, at any age, or whatever is our heaviest burden when death impacts our lives, we do have to go on. Even without the time I was blessed with, I would have eventually moved forward. Not likely as quickly to the place I am now, but I would have done what I needed to do as a person, as a mother, what she would have wanted me to do, what she would have done.

Regardless of comparisons and gratitude, the reality is that her death has created a gaping hole in my world. But without doubt, I feel her at peace because I am moving beyond that, beyond myself as my focus and creating a positive outcome rather than agonising over it and letting it hold me down. I still need her, but she benefits when I keep our relationship alive and manage without her.

It's such a strange mix of knowing that she is there any time I need her and even times when I don't, while also feeling so deeply alone. She is "there" for me, but not "here", but I know in my heart that when I miss her, she is right by my side. Arlyn might be right; she is the one who "has it pretty good", although I think, despite being with me more than she was ever able to be before, she misses me, too.

So, these days, I don't mind her "breathing down my neck all the time". She sits beside me as I write this book. She watches me and shares herself with me while I help organise and decorate Orla's birthday party or give Arlyn advice about friendships. She is giving me a hug while I struggle with issues with my job, which helps me to believe that there is something bigger, more exciting, and financially rewarding out there for me. She is often laughing with me, "showing off" to me. Proving to me that she is still there by doing those things quite often at the same time.

A good example of this happened about a month after she died. I was cleaning the house, listening to a podcast on grief as I worked. I was in a light mood, enjoying the sunshine, but as is often the case, was quietly shedding missing-her tears. Housework days like those were when I would usually call her to catch up, and we would talk for hours, often for the entire school day. I was dusting the shelf around the box of Mum's ashes, having a little laugh with her about dusting around her dust. The podcast was talking about manifesting signs. Everything from butterflies to sloths was mentioned as proof that loved ones hadn't gone far. I believe in the afterlife and without any doubt believe in signs, so I'm not necessarily a sceptic, but I have always been a tough customer; neither an easily impressed nor easily led person, I guess you'd say.

As I listened, I thought, *There's no way I'd be happy with a butterfly as my sign, that would be far too inconclusive, far too cliché.*

Butterflies are common (although Orla had an experience I'll mention later that changed my perception of the simplicity of that idea). If you need reassurance from a sign, why choose the classic butterfly? I had the specific thought that perhaps they seem magical because they are pretty, but that they are as common as a fly or a bug, yet nobody seems to choose those as their signs.

Laughing at how harsh and critical I can be, I became aware of something tickling my head and then heard a loud buzzing and felt something flapping, caught in my hair. I violently shook my head, flicking my hair, and out flew an abnormally large fly-like creature! Definitely a fly, but unlike one I have ever seen. March Fly in size but a different colour and shape. It flew across my lounge room into a window track. Instantly aware that the fly had arrived out of nowhere, just as I was having the thought about a fly being a sign instead of a butterfly, I knew this was not a coincidence. I had an intensely strange interaction with that fly, lasting about an hour that morning. It would go on to disappear, then reappear over the next three days.

I heard it buzzing from the kitchen window magically one morning immediately after I finished telling the girls about the circumstances of its arrival, my experiences with it, and how I believed it was Mimi playing with me, and not only showing me she was with me, but that I wasn't as smart as I thought I was because even something "ordinary" like a fly can prove magic is around.

Without persuasion, it climbed from the windowsill onto my hand (it was the same fly; its size and markings were distinctive), and we took it outside. The three of us spent well over half an hour with it (her), talking to it, laughing, and taking photos with it in the garden, passing it between us as it stepped with its tiny fly legs from hand to hand rather than flying off, despite showing no signs of injury. Eventually, we placed it on a rock to leave it be, the girls regularly checking on it for over an hour before discovering it had finally gone.

A different, strange variety of fly-like insect that I've never seen before (re)appeared to me on the beach a few weeks later for another interesting interaction. I had gone there specifically to sit with my sadness, feeling desperate to see Mum, I'd requested that she "prove" herself to me there as a dolphin (which I have never spotted from that particular beach). So, as was her way in life, in death, she teaches me profound and new things through humour. She "proves" her wizardry to me in ways that are not straightforward. So, I am never alone (and I have yet to see a dolphin from that beach).

She has, on many occasions since the magical magnet butterfly episode and the "fly encounter", shown me more of her powers, filling me with hope, happiness, and gratitude. One afternoon, a few months after she died, we went to the beach for a barbie for dinner. Watching dogs running around in the off-leash section, Orla said she wished she could bring Lexi to the beach (Lexi, I am sure, does not share that desire), lamenting that she didn't think it fair that dogs get to go out with their owners, but cats don't. No longer had she finished her sentence when we noticed a couple walking directly towards us from the water with a cat on a lead! I have heard of people taking a cat for a walk. I've never seen it, although apparently it is "a thing", but on the beach? A dog beach?!

While we all laughed, Arlyn piped up with, "I think that was Mimi! Mimi made that cat be here, because that seemed like magic." I agreed but mentioned that even if it wasn't Mimi, she would enjoy getting the credit. As soon as I said that, a small mixed breed dog, a very unusual looking dog, ran towards us from the same direction as the cat walkers and started spinning around right in front of us, making us all laugh yet again, and as who we assumed to be its owners approached, they started calling it to come back to them — "Mimi. Mimi. Come here, Mim" (Mim was Arlyn's nickname for Mum).

I thought, *Are they saying Minnie?* I listened carefully, no, *Mimi.* The dog's name was Mimi.

Okay, Mum. Got it. You are there, it is you, and you are indeed very tricky!

Aside from this obvious showing off, I feel her quietly (and sometimes loudly) by my side as I work with her, finishing poems she started, we listen to music together, or as I discipline the girls or enjoy long, warm cuddles with them. Right from the beginning, she started "making" me rub things as a sign that she was there. The way she was rubbing the rose quartz in palliative care, the way she used to rub her fingers against her fingernails, or any smooth item she might have in her hand. I find myself doing that now on things like the remote or my fingernails, and I know it's her "proving herself", reminding me that she is with me. I hear her wisecracks and comforting, reassuring answers when we have our little chats about everyday things. We share lots of laughs, maybe more so than ever. I can feel her being proud of both my everyday accomplishments and times when I get it wrong, but try harder next time. I feel her enjoyment in watching me read and her happiness about the genre of books I'm gravitating towards. Some are books she long ago recommended, but I either wasn't ready for or wasn't interested in, because the recommendation had come from her, and my attitude meant I figured they might be a bit crap.

I'm sure she was elated watching over our family respond to her death with such unity, depth, and humour. I know in the months afterwards that the support I received from Jude and my cousins via a messenger chat group that I would often wake to find 147 unread messages on, was as much of a comfort to her as it was to me. Although we were already close, it was talking about Mum that enabled the connection in our group to really develop and flourish with some of my cousins, and deepen to a new level with others. The support I received from my close and wider friendship circles, and even knowing where I stand with those who could be perceived as letting me down, has also been a gift for both of us. Mum doesn't have to see me struggling along on my own and is enjoying the lessons I have now learnt on responding to someone else's loss and grief, so that I don't make those same unintended or totally disregarded, unempathetic mistakes myself.

Despite all of this, I am left feeling sad. Of course, I am sad. My mum died, and as a result, I now feel like I've got all of this wisdom and compassion for her, and we don't really get to share either. But I can't dwell on that. There are so many other feelings and thoughts to process. She is dead. I can't change that. Instead, I can easily focus on things like how lucky I was to spend so many years with her, to have had *her* as my mum in the first place. She was a big believer in the concept that children choose their parents. If this is true, I'm proud of myself for choosing so well. I had a Mum who raised me to be able to recognise my blessings, be able to rely on myself, see the humour in *everything* and see an opportunity to grow as a result of the hardest thing I've ever experienced. I got to be there while she processed her death and when she died. How can I stagnate in grief, regret or guilt, when those feelings are so intrinsically linked with gratitude, and relief that at least her death has not been for nothing? It is serving such a massive purpose. It is the catalyst for the "sequel" to the book that is my life.

Presumably, timed perfectly mid-way through my existence here on earth (timing is everything). Part two — my life without Mum here doesn't have to be filled with tales of doom and gloom. It's the volume where the self-reflection started in part one, when I became a mother, that really takes flight. Life and death are both miracles that hold so many opportunities for growth on so many complex levels.

In my limited experience of death, I have found that it shares so many similarities with birth. The very first time you *see* your newborn child. The first time you have real space to share the moment of looking at each other, to stare right into the depths of each other's eyes, you are filled with love that seems to overpower your capacity to feel anything else. I feel that I need to mention here, as it was in my case, that as that sacred initial moment settles within you, you can also be filled with panic.

An overwhelming feeling of anxiety and heavy responsibility that often seems to be overlooked or not mentioned because love is the thing you are expecting and expected to feel. But despite that intense pressure, love is undoubtedly there. It is the thing that causes the insecurity. The love may be instant and totally blissful, or it may take time to develop, but it is there. Then you go on to commence your life with that child. To feed it, bathe it, keep it warm or cool, and you live life in a bubble of what's right in front of you. You seldom think of things like teething in a few months or he or she throwing a massive tantrum at the shops in a few years, let alone struggling with friendships, rebelling, first heartbreak, or any of the things that make a life real. There is a period of time where it is just "newborn hard" because it is new and so all-consuming, but it is also "newborn magic", pure and wonder-filled.

When someone you love dies, maybe in particular when that someone is your mother, you can go through a similar thing. Depending on the relationship, of course, but if you did have a solid bond, you can be kicked in the guts with how much love you have. Even though it was always there and even if it was always acknowledged, it's a much more intense version of love than you may have felt, actually *felt*, rather than just known was in the background, while she was alive. Like the beginning of parenthood, you have "new death hard" as you struggle with things you hadn't considered or had any ability to actually know until she died. While you feel the anxiety or the realisation of how hard it is, you also swim in the bubble of how wonderful she was, just as your newborn was. You have "new death magic".

As your newborn grows, the love never stops, but it changes. You have times when you are filled with anger, regret, or even disappointment. Life outside the newborn magic bubble is real, which isn't to say inside it is not, but it doesn't stay that way forever.

When Mum first died, the module of the "new death bubble" was real. But as time goes on, life outside it is where you eventually find yourself. You can't live in that bubble forever; it's unsustainable. It is designed to burst. It sounds like a harsh way to say it, but the novelty of birth and death eventually wears off. You go forward, living new experiences with the no longer newborn — the toddler, the primary school years and so on, and you're not constantly in awe of your child every hour of the day. In a similar but reverse way, when someone you love dies, it's like you've got a fresh bubble. Then your life keeps unfolding, but instead of new experiences, you have memories to process. It will always be all of those same years and same events, but you are living them via "reliving" them.

On top of that, you are constantly aware that as all of your new experiences happen, that person is not there, and that's forever more. Your person, who has always been in all your lifetime's worth of experiences, doesn't know that part. All of that can make you feel stuck, trapped inside. Or as has been the case for me, the bubble pops and shakes you out, eventually.

In the months after she died, Mum became almost a perfect person to me. My grief gifted me with a narrow focus on how brightly she shone. I think I really needed that perspective of appreciation. Like "newborn magic", the purity of the gift of that person is all that you see in front of you, like the story hasn't unfolded yet. Instead of the fear of the newborn bubble, sadness shadows closely alongside. Initially, for me, love and wonder overpowered everything; my reaction to her house in the days after her death is a good example of this. Ultimately, though, life unfolds. While it does, with love still as the dominant force, you are able to see things differently. The *experience* of love settles, enabling you to *feel* and understand the reality of all that the person and your relationship with them had, and continues to offer you. Grief is the thing that differentiates the two ends of the spectrum of birth and death. You don't always seem to take the same time to deeply reflect while you are travelling through life with the person, unfortunately. When you lose someone, grief offers a new opportunity to do so. Grief is there in place of new direct experiences with that person.

Perhaps in part due to my burdening gift of regret reminding me to see things from a wider vantage point, as my day-to-day life kept unfolding, I began to reorganise my feelings and memories. As that reality continues to expand, I am aware that I am seeing the world more and more as she did. I can feel myself becoming more like her, and I am embracing it in a way I possibly wouldn't have yet if she were still alive.

I find myself remembering something that happened and thinking, *Geez, Mum was such a pain about that.* That wasn't happening when I was in the "new death bubble". I wasn't ready for that. She was only perfect to me then, but I now see her with more clarity. With that comes a deeper understanding as to why she might have behaved that way. Her responses were perhaps sometimes because of her flaws, but she was also responding to an imperfect world, with imperfect relationships in it. I always knew she was a good mum, that I loved her, that she was a pretty cool chick. But I also noticed her faults and gave her that feedback far too often. She used to call me on it. She was confident in herself and in her mothering, despite it.

She must have known I'd catch up one day. Now, I am able to reflect on all that she offered me and feel happy that I am so much like her, while still being proud of who I am in ways we are different. I am learning that some of her flaws were actually *my* responses to her. Sadly, or perhaps not, her death teaches me all of that. Mum wasn't perfect, but she *always* prioritised our happiness. Her children were the thing that kept her alive, quite literally, in times when I know she was suffering with extreme depression, and the thought of getting the fuck out of here felt like a much better option. But she didn't, because of us. She literally lived for us. But now she's free, floating around out there somewhere, anywhere she wants to be, still being Mum. Still guiding me with her now angelic ways, enjoying her afterlife, the new version of her existence, while I am here, enjoying the shining light of our new relationship, but also feeling the darkness of not giving her more of what she needed. Light and shade in life, but only light in death.

Regret. My curse and my blessing. It grounds me. It means that I am not let off the hook to alter history and pretend that everything was perfect. Without it, I would miss the lessons that its darkness offers me. I know I could have done better, but with regret comes self-reflection. That reflection bounces off the regret and creates the new light that we are now sharing, and that is helping to shape this better version of myself that I know I am becoming. That I like becoming. Even if I don't like that she had to die for it to be this way, maybe that's just too bad. Pain has opened me up to receive just as much, if not more than it has taken from me.

I know I wouldn't be the person I am today if I weren't a mother; maybe it's a similar thing? Perhaps I needed to lose my mother to develop in this way? I am deeply certain that her death, be,ng the death it was, is the key that opens that door. Had she suffered a harder death or died without me there to help her, I am sure I wouldn't have the capacity for this same level of growth. Maybe I would have gotten there eventually, but I feel it is more likely that I would still be drowning in regret.

Thankfully, our relationship was solid. Thankfully, I got time to say goodbye.

Those two things are so important and are part of the reason I can use the regret so constructively, I guess, and really value it. I feel I owe her the acknowledgment of regret. It has no place in our new relationship but serves as a good yardstick of how far we've come. It also reminds me that it's never too late to make amends, and our relationship continues. I still give her cheek and hear her comebacks (I know exactly what she would be saying, so we're *still* fighting for the last word!). My regret is a heavy load, but when I see her again, it will be gone. I won't honour it anymore. We can just cruise around in the pure light, side by side, grateful that our relationship got there regardless of where each of us was at the time.

Accepting regret shifts my perspective on many things from being a curse to a blessing. Initially, and even to some extent still now, death made life seem very "bland". The sneak peek I had through that door meant that, comparatively, life lost a bit of its "shine" for me. Witnessing Mum's death and experiencing the heavy grief of the first few months was a time of enlightenment. It was like I was given backstage access to a beautiful show. Watching her in the spotlight from the darkness of the wings, but so close to the action. Because it was someone I love so dearly starring in the show, I was directly invested in it, yet still able to share the wider gift that the story was providing the audience. Afterwards, when the curtain closed and the lights were turned off, on some level, I felt like I had lost a bit of interest or perspective on the gift that is life. That experience was so intense, so inspiring, that nothing could compete. The show was over, and it felt like a bit of a letdown to just go home and live.

Feeling that way made me not only reflect on my own life, but on life in general. I felt, and still in some ways feel, jaded about how crap things are so often here on earth. We do wrong by each other so often. We value the wrong things. Our goals, relationships, possessions, and experiences, all of which are precious things, all of which are certainly worth living for, are only so if we are consciously allowing love to guide us. But so often, although externally we look like we're going forward, we are actually just going through the motions. It seems we either live life with no regard for death or are fearful of it in a way that serves no purpose. Understanding death from the perspective of an afterlife and allowing death the space to inform our choices from a place of depth, rather than just looking externally and kidding ourselves that we are "living our best lives", means that death and life are of equal value.

Losing Mum has blessed me with the realisation that the "real deal" is the afterlife. In my experience, the curse of death is also the blessing of introspection. Death is no longer an abstract concept. It is a gift that makes me more aware of using my life phase to construct the best version of who I can be. The circular aspect of that is that when I die, my legacy is more in line with what I hope it to be.

Maybe sometimes the reason I feel so negative about life or the high levels of bullshit all of us carry on with and endure is that I just miss Mum so deeply that I would easily leave it all behind to be with her again, regardless of how genuinely magical or talked up life is to be. To be able to be together in a place free of any of the burdens we experience in this existence seems like a double win.

Make no mistake, I'm not talking about being suicidal; I value my life, but the experience I had makes me value death equally. The context of her death is key, not just the fact that she is dead. I may have been too wounded to make peace with it had it happened differently. Being closer to death than I ever have been and seeing grief as my ally has profoundly changed the way I see everything. It isn't as simplistic as making sure I live each day to the fullest, squeezing the best I can out of my very blessed existence. I do feel that way in a sense, I guess, but the gift of being there and it being as much as possible, on her own terms, has calmed me down rather than inspiring me to view life as this entity that should be respected above all else.

Of course, that doesn't detract from the gratitude I have for things like my health, or my family's health, and doesn't stop me from wanting to do everything in my power to make sure my kids have a happy and safe life now and ahead. Naturally, while I'm here, I'd like to see amazing things, enjoy myself, do things that make me proud, ensure my kids have positive experiences and guide them as they develop in all the years they have ahead to be the best that they can be. But while I am doing all of that, I am always aware that this is just "level one".

The purpose of living is so much more about self-reflection, learning how you can best serve yourself and others, rather than just filling it with big, loud events. Sure, create, plan, and enjoy your time, create beautiful memories and a meaningful legacy, but also allow room for that to just flow naturally. Make sure you are slowed down enough to process and appreciate even the most basic things that we may not even see as being experiences or goals. Living should be so much more integrated with the next stage, rather than feeling almost complacent about how important life is, because I've got a sneaking suspicion that it gets much better from here.

For those who have done their best (maybe even for those who haven't?), the real gift comes when you die. There is so much to be anxious about here, so much to keep your mind busy. So much to feel sad about. People punch elderly people and sexually abuse children for fucks sake! So much evil exists that it breaks my heart and wears me down sometimes. Things like that happen, you could say for seemingly no logical reason, although the reason or link is another thing that burdens my thoughts, but it just is what it is; that's how life is.

A way of managing that heaviness is to understand life as a mixture of light and darkness so that when we die, we recognise the difference. Maybe that's why people say they see such a bright light when they're dying, because there is no darkness "there" at all. Here, darkness can have its own beauty. We can even see the magnificence of it through little pin pricks and bigger holes of light poking through to comfort and amaze us, but only if we take the time to stop, go out and look up. If we do, we can figure out how to appreciate the darkness. We seem to know or accept that our soul needs it. It is "part of life". Then, eventually, or for some people after no time at all (perhaps because they don't need to be bothered with that lesson), we get to walk into the beaming brightness and never have to deal with the hardship and bullshit that darkness can also create.

When we go, we will realise so little was a big deal. That we should've had our eye on the prize more, lived the breathing existence with more awareness of how trivial so much about our time here is. We'll realise the importance of stuff that we're not even noticing. In many ways, we totally disregard the significance death has in every single one of our lives. We are so fearful of it, so uncomfortable talking about where we're all eventually heading. We try to ignore it, which means we forget to plan for it with any real depth and, in doing so, forget to get to know ourselves and get to know others without all the nonsense getting in the way.

We don't get excited, as weird as that may sound, about the most amazing destination we can all afford to go to. We all get a free ticket! It's a place we certainly don't need to rush to get to, but when we apply stillness and purpose on this level, perhaps we can see more so as our gift rather than such a negative thing. It may be the best place we'll ever go and the best experience we'll ever have.

Mum's dying, her death too, but more so her dying, has helped make me more humble and more grateful that those "big deal" things about life have lost some of their power over me. That's what I mean by some of the "shine" being taken away. Rather than the light being dimmed, now the light of life shines in completely different directions, shining outwardly from me, rather than feeling like I am, or should be, in the spotlight.

"Ours" is a dying story that can easily be seen as a blessing; we really were fortunate. It was not a death that was overly drawn out (despite my exhausted impatience). She has many health issues, but she didn't suffer through a long illness or a life-long condition that caused intense physical and or mental agony. I am not grieving the death of my child of any age. I don't have to suffer the death of a parent or someone who fulfils that role, from a child's perspective. I have not experienced death due to violence or neglect. Although initially I was in shock, I was gifted time to process the impending death and the ability to be there when it happened, rather than having no warning. I didn't find out my loved one was dying somewhere I couldn't get to. It wasn't the result of wrongdoing or something done purposefully, through negligence, or a stupid, avoidable mistake. I am not dealing with the devastation and shock caused by the deaths of multiple loved ones in a single instance. COVID did not impact us in the variety of horrific ways it did for so many others facing a similar situation to ours. I do not have to go through this life searching for positivity or a reason to go on while dealing with the fact that my loved one died alone, or in any way that was traumatic or frightening for them. I have certainty about her love; my mother didn't emotionally, or otherwise, injure me, so I don't have to process it in a way that is isolating.

My loss is relatable. I didn't have to sit beside my person with animosity, or regretting lost time within my control or otherwise. My family was tight, but we bonded more so as a result; losing her didn't fracture any of my relationships.

Despite her pure heart, Mum didn't die because this existence was so hard that she took herself to the next one on purpose. Until the day before, her cognition was perfect, so I know she knew I was there. Because of all of that and more, I was able to laugh and to process and come through the other side knowing that I had done my best for her in her dying, even if I hadn't always done so in her living. That helps ease my pain or regret. All of those alternatives make a huge difference to my ongoing responses to facing the fact that she died.

My mum died. She was too young, and I am too young. My mum died after having to lie on her hard kitchen floor, enduring what is medically referred to as a "long lie", which, although succinctly and accurately worded, is a phrase that makes my stomach churn. She suffered, alone, in the heat, wondering if she would be found, if anyone was registering her existence. Lying in her urine and faeces, feeling and smelling that, while it damaged her skin because she couldn't move out of it. She slowly started dying from a stroke and a heart attack that no one knew she had suffered. That is a difficult reality to swallow.

Imagining my mum there, knowing that she was one of "those people" who experienced that, makes me feel sorrow and shame. It certainly wasn't "ideal"; I loathe that part of the story. I know I will never be okay with it. But she didn't die there. My mum died in a bed with enough medication to keep her comfortable, surrounded by the people she loved most, after days of hearing our laughter and knowing perhaps more than she had ever known, that she was cherished. Although she certainly put in some hard yards, she died with dignity. She died a death that she deserved rather than one that matched the life she had led, where she wasn't always understood or treated with respect. She had always carried herself with the knowledge that this level was not the "real deal". She wasn't really made for this existence. That level, that place, was where she was always going to be allowed to shine her brightest.

Chapter 13 – Gifts

With all this talk of gratitude, self-reflection, and growth, I do want to make it clear to anyone reading who doesn't relate, or perceives some of what I am saying as a seemingly full of laughs, glowing report of how inspiring and positive it is to get to watch your mum die, that it was traumatic, and will always cause me pain. But it's a beautiful kind of pain that I am happy to carry as both a burden and a means of giving me strength. I am certain that I don't have the level of anguish I would have if Mum suffered any more than she did, died alone, or any of those other options. My experience provides me with a truer sense of empathy for those, both living and dead, who have had those experiences.

Through her death, I have been gifted a level of multifaceted gratitude that I couldn't get any other way. My grieving can flow more easily because Mum died the way she did. My life is richer because I got to witness the mess and experience the suffering the way that I did. The regrets I have about our relationship are eased a little because we shared what we shared in the end, freeing me of an otherwise unmanageable burden, not just caused by her having had a horrible death, but also by how overwhelmed I would feel about her having a hard life and the part I played in not helping her life be more joyful or comfortable.

I could choose to look at it as being too little, too late. But I don't. Mum wouldn't want me to. She knows what we shared was always solid and special, and that her death didn't create that, but she is enjoying our relationship, still developing and improving, so it's never too late.

If I filled myself with regret and total anguish, there wouldn't be as much room for the gifts we now share. I would rob us *both* of that, but as a mother myself, I am so happy that I am not taking that away from *her*. That completely open connection and depth of love and understanding with your child is every mother's wish. I know she would never leave me anyway, so why would it be too late? We can go forward building a new relationship, one that I will never know if we would have had, had it not been for those few days by her side. So, because I am left with no choice, I must value her death. Rather than being consumed by physically losing her, I recognise the immense importance of being there and that she went in peace, allowing me to grieve but also move forward with her, as best as I am able. I am switched on to something that I could never have accessed otherwise. I am more whole. I *feel* more.

I am aware of slowing my thinking down so that I can process, not just race through my apparent "awareness" of things in what was really an unconscious way. I am "quieter". I'm being led somewhere by someone I can trust. I can surrender, lean into life, and more easily see beyond its pressures. Maybe that's one of the many gifts you get when you are being both guarded and guided by an angel. Part of their job in watching over you is to encourage you to "release" so you can feel their wings whispering in your heart, rather than hearing all the external shouting in your ears and mind.

I am sure that, regardless of the child's age, it's possible for mothers to continue to guide their children after their death, but I acknowledge that, among other things, the time I had with Mum allows me to feel her presence in a way I would likely be unaware of if I had not known her. So, for me, who was blessed on both accounts of being a mother and knowing my mother, grief sometimes feels like a "labour of love".

I am lucky to have gone through "labour" in a reverse, but strangely similar, way to the way she did for me at birth.

She gave me the "gift of life". I gave her the "gift of death". Both are hard things to do, but also absolutely jammed packed with beauty, and both create the start of something new. Birth facilitates life. Death doesn't eradicate the life; the person still exists, not just through memories of people they lived with and loved, but *within* them.

We continue to build relationships as we traverse all that being born, living, dying, and grieving have to offer. She was there for me in the beginning. I was there for her at the end. She held all the hopes and dreams for me; I hold all the grief for her. That doesn't have to be a "stuck" or negative thing. Life and grief are both fluid and can facilitate new opportunities and experiences.

It feels to me like there are many more layers to death and grief than they get credit for, that it is both sides of the life and afterlife spectrums that reach so far.

Mum gave her parents the gift of grandchildren. Those grandchildren then went on to provide them the gift of being there for their child at her death, in a way that they alone couldn't be, so that she was being supported from "both sides". Although Mum's death was untimely, both she and I were blessed that at least we worked in that order, unlike Nanna and others like her, who endured the pain of the death of a child, (my beautiful uncle, Michael).

Mum and I lost our mothers as grown women, old enough to use death as a tool, whereas in her lifetime, Nanna lost both a child and a mother, and not only was she just a child at the time of her mother Ena's death, but it was handled in such a way that caused her tremendous confusion and unnecessary suffering.

Nanna losing her mother at her age and in the way she did created so much turmoil for her to grow up in. I believe that seeing Mum and me labouring through her death together would've been such a blessing to her, despite me swearing at her and demanding she somehow get it over and done with!

It really is similar to birthing in that way — swearing, pleading, and mess. Nanna obviously had the insight to know I needed that hard labour, and after all, Mum had gone through that for me. In her wisdom, she gave us both

the credit that we could handle it, and she allowed Mum
to direct things instead of stepping in and taking that gift
away from us too quickly. The threads of Nanna's mother-
and-child loss will forever run through our family, and
although she certainly wouldn't have contemplated a birth
plan for Mum's birth (aside from getting the cows milked
first), she certainly mapped out a very good "death plan" for
her from her afterlife vantage point.

Death seems to result in introspection for those left
behind. When there is a depth of connection, whether positive
or not, that may happen quickly, or it may take time, and
while it ebbs and flows, it never ever goes away. Reflection
takes us back and moves us forward; the beginning and
ending meet in the middle and form a circle. A circle of life
and death.

When someone we care for dies, love may also
facilitate intense wonder. Through that, we could
understand grief as going back to the beginning. At the
start of the story with our loved one, we are gifted love
that fills us with expectation and anticipation in all their
variations, and time is irrelevant to how deeply we feel
those feelings. Whether we loved someone for 10 days, 9
months, or 50 years, and irrespective of if we ever met, or
can remember them, when someone dies, we often reflect
on those emotions. Instead of that ending, grief can be a
tool to help us come back to that reflection. Grief is pure
love. Grief keeps the person "alive". Therefore, grief can
take us back to the start; we could use it to consider,
*"What will I do with this albeit unwanted, but new version of our
relationship?"*. Half a circle rocks from side to side, or falls
flat; both sides are required to keep things turning. My
grief keeps her here. It is the key that keeps that circle
spinning, keeps me finding joy in our relationship, and
keeps me implementing the lessons she was banging on
about for all of those years.

One of the lessons she did manage to get through to
me was the importance of respecting and tending to the
bonds of family. The circular connection of grief shaping
new experiences is illustrated by how our wider family
responded to Mum's death. Sharing our grief renewed an

acknowledgment of how much we love and want to support each other.

Mum and those in the whistle choir calling her to join them came together in the ultimate white light, but we also responded to that call. When it came to darkness, we rallied together to create our own shiny yellow light here, too, and they were a part of that. The tangible presence of a person is, of course, *really* important. You never get over that loss. You will never, ever, find that okay, but grief demonstrates that the person's life doesn't die with their body. You *can* take them forward with you; they do not have to be "missing", you do not have to be 'left behind". By keeping life and death intertwined, keeping the circle spinning, you can create new memories with them *through* them, rather than just living with their memory or the idea of what may have been.

Grief links before and after. It is the middle piece that creates the bridge. When the loss is related to something we never got to experience, or even something that failed to meet our expectations, like a relationship, a lifestyle, a dream we yearned for that was never fulfilled, that grief can be a total burden. That link is understandably not always a welcome one. We may wish we had never encountered that bridge, let alone been forced to walk on it. But when it is caused by someone we love dying, no matter how long we loved them, that word, with its negative connotation, "grief", is not something we would want to *not* have. Without it, the link is gone, and we don't ever want that to be the case. We don't want to not grieve, and "move on". The link honours them. We may feel that we can't get to the other side, stuck in the middle of the bridge, afraid, desperate, unable to keep walking across, but we have the foundations of that bridge to steady us. The bridge was built by love, so its footings are very strong. We built the bridge together.

I said earlier that *I* gave her "the gift of death", which is a very simplistic way to see it. In fact, she gave *me* gifts of life, of her death, *and* of my own death. I now see life and death as of equal importance, so I view the "gift of life" as stretching far beyond that expression.

Apparently, life is the gift, and while death is intrinsically in that mix, it's usually overlooked. I really look forward to my life progressing, but also to my afterlife, so I have Mum to thank for both. Without her, the myriads of those physical and spiritual paths wouldn't exist for me. My safe entry into this world, the care she provided and attention to my every need are her most obvious gifts to me. But the evolving awakening her death has ignited that now helps me along with my living, is without doubt yet another, let alone the transcendent wonders that await me when my own time comes. The experience of us guiding each other during her dying, her "role modelling" while being so open to my input, giving me the space and the strength to endure both her dying and her death and raising me with concepts and therefore skills to manage afterwards, are all gifts only she could give. She has taught me not to fear, that I can look forward to my own transition. Her valuable lessons seem to be never-ending.

The mother-daughter relationship is unique, regardless of whether it's a negative or positive bond, so it is a specific type of grief. Even if the case is that the mother is alive, but lost due to memory or cognition issues, physical separation, or abandonment, or is emotionally absent in terms of support, stability, or love, the loss of a mother shapes you.

Along my grief journey, it has occurred to me how life-defining it must be to miss someone you didn't know or can't remember. Ripples of the dumping, crashing waves that losing a parent at a young age can create last a lifetime, and beyond, impacting the next generation in a way that would not have been the case if it weren't for that missing thread. It must be such a strange "longing", so ingrained, *embedded*, rather than just mentally comprehended.

Although how and who you grieve is an individual experience and there is no hierarchy as such, one of the heaviest losses is surely that of a child, no matter their age and regardless of how that child came to be "yours". With specific reference to birth mothers, I imagine that part of grief is a response to having once shared a body; your soul knows you were once one. I felt a version of that physical loss when Mum died, like an actual part of me was no longer able to be accessed; an amputation of sorts. In that way, I believe the outcomes of Mum's death will not be replicated in any future death experiences I will endure. Hopefully, aside from my own, when I die with my adult daughters by my side.

I am so lucky that in my case, my relationship with Mum was one of the good ones. That she was the holder of so much information about me. Now that I have children of my own, I realise she probably knew me better than I did. She knew all the little "secret spaces", let alone the stories, and took memories of me that I will never know about. She watched me grow while she grew too, as a direct result of that. Our individual development was fed by each other. I'm so grateful that both of us got to have that as our life's story, rather than being torn away from each other earlier than we were.

I had a sudden realisation when walking through the bakery section in Woollies one day, that she is the only person who knows I really like bee sting bun. She would buy it for me in lieu of a birthday cake, and despite other people being at those parties, I'm certain no one registered. Unless I now specifically make that known, no one else in the world knows that about me. It seems silly, but it overwhelms me sometimes that those kinds of details about me are lost. Fighting a losing battle against my tears as I tried to finish my groceries, I realised I'm now the only one who knows that secret, unimportant information that she made seem important, let alone the things about my life story that no one knows now, not even me. But she has given me so much, genetically and through her nurturing, so much of me is her that what was once just bee sting bun knowledge is something that now runs so deep that she can work through me, enabling me to climb up and out of the well of grief. To surface from its miserable depths, to begin to thrive with death and grief as my guide and companion, rather than my enemy.

Aside from realising how much I look like her as the years pass, I'm also increasingly relating to her, which isn't to say I agree with everything she did and said, but I see now that many of our differences of opinion came from my judgments and high expectations of her. I didn't see myself as always being in the right; rather, that she shouldn't get things wrong. I am proud of her for defending her right to be just who she was. Through examining our similarities, I can learn from her mistakes, but not from a harsh or critical perspective. She is softening me.

Her death and living with the regret of my unrealistic demands of how it should be is clearly not an ideal way to have to do it, but my guilt serves me. It's heavy, but most big tools are. Maybe I would've started on this path without having to physically lose her to do so, maybe my maturity would've gotten me there eventually, I'll never know, but she taught me to reflect, and I know for certain that she is using her newly formed powers to help me see her in my mirror. To a degree, I was doing so before she died, but in retrospect, I wasn't acting on it. Her death has put me back on the path of self-assessment I embarked on when I first had my children, and she would be very happy about that. That's the type of thing she was always into, "hippy", self-development stuff that other mums didn't seem to crap on about. In my younger years, that used to annoy the shit out of me, but now, it's another important lesson of hers that eventually got through.

As I learn to respond externally to these introspective reflections, I am able to make peace with her untimely death because, although it was cut short, I had time to get to know her as an adult. Even without her here to physically learn from, she packed so much teaching in "telling me what to do all the time", so much of *her* in me, that I know I am fortunate to have gotten to a point in my life where I have the beginnings of a skillset to manage living without her.

She can sit back and not have to deal with me whinging about her imparting her knowledge and know that I am actually grateful for it. She can enjoy me grappling with our similarities and differences, rather than us fighting because we were so strongly both. Maybe as the years roll on, I'll just organically become more like her. Perhaps I'll consciously do things differently, too. But despite my deep sorrow about losing her wisdom as a sounding board through all those useful discussions or arguments, even, I know our connection and love are deep enough that sadness will never overpower her ability to continue helping me, especially now that I am more open to listening.

One night, about 12 months after she died, I dreamt she came back to life. It is the only dream I have had about her since her death. It was one of those very clear dreams that you'd swear was real. The intensity of the relief and joy was immense, and my response to her resurrection was initially all that you would expect, yet the dream played out with me quickly moving through that miracle with a total lack of insight, living life as I actually had when she was alive. I found myself back to my old ways of taking her for granted, and although I was aware that I was doing so, I kept making no effort, kept prioritising everything else that I knew was not as important, and despite being in total disbelief about and furious and disgusted by my behaviour, that continued day after day. I woke up knowing she had sent me that dream, totally her style, but that it was a lesson about how I live my life rather than specifically about her death or our relationship. Perhaps it is because I can still hear her, maybe I just know her so well, but I know why I haven't been gifted dreams like that before or since. She dropped in that night as a reminder, but she would also be saying, "I am here for you, my shiny girl, but it is actually up to you to learn from your mistakes with action, rather than just insight."

The timing of that dream was no coincidence. In the 12 months after she died, missing her filled every aspect of my life; I actively connected with her in a way that I loved because it included all of life's colours. Yet as time progresses, I often drift back to old patterns of turning to her more for help rather than including her in the good or ordinary moments. I am aware that I wish more desperately for her to be alive again when shit gets hard or even slightly uncomfortable. It shows me that she was the only person I've ever and will ever depend on to such depth. She was both the soft pillow to cry into and the secure, reliable, hard cement post to lean up against, and cry and lean hard I did.

Although I am ashamed to admit it, her death was the catalyst that made me finally act on that. My dream was sent for many reasons, one being a little kick up the arse to help me stop doing that. It's another demonstration that I'm still learning from her in an active way, that I still want to improve our relationship as it continues to evolve.

Assessing myself as a daughter in such ways brings me so much insight into my role as a mother, particularly highlighting, with a big fat yellow pen, the similarities between my relationship with Mum and my relationship with Orla. I am immensely proud of Orla in a way that is completely independent of anything I have done raising her. With an always open heart, she quietly perseveres, learning to cope in a world that doesn't adequately value those with sensitive dispositions like hers. I am in awe of how she doesn't adapt to that world; rather, she holds true to who she is and walks confidently forward on her own path, always with deep kindness towards herself and others, traits she got from Mum.

I am learning through Mum's death that I often respond to those beautiful traits with anxiety, even frustration, the same way I did to Mum. Mum was often exhausted by the constant strain of maintaining her softness in the loud and often harsh world we live in, something Orla also struggles with. So often, I judged their inevitable breaking point moments as a lack of resilience or being "too sensitive". I did have some insight that I was doing that with Mum, but until she died, I wasn't as aware that I was also doing so to Orla.

Of course, what Orla needs during such times is support rather than judgement. It feels as though Mum has teamed up with Orla to help me learn this, so that my guilt about misunderstanding my mother does not have to be replicated with my daughter. In that way, their relationship has also evolved since Mum's death, as on a spiritual level, they are working together for a purpose that serves us all.

I have been gifted two beautiful daughters who are, in almost every way, polar opposites. At only a few days old, it was evident to me that Arlyn's disposition included a high level of easy to measure resiliency. Through stories told to me by Mum, and my own memories, I know that my resilience was learnt, and wasn't, in any way, easy for me to develop. Yet, despite Orla's innate self-confidence and emotional depth, and despite being anxious by nature myself, I have always been impatient with Orla learning to manage difficulties and overlooked the ways she applies her version of doing so.

What I have perceived to be a lack of resilience and "day-dreamy ways" has somehow resulted in me having expectations of her that disregard her strengths and instead put pressure on her to be someone she is not; someone who gets on with it, rather than someone who allows herself the space she readily and rightly tells me she needs and deserves. This response parallels my disapproving attitude towards Mum. The way I perceived her as having an inability to get over being separated from Sam and me when we were young, and the treatment she received from Dad and Jo, or anyone who treated her with disrespect. Despite also knowing that she endured so much and that she was no pushover, somehow, overall, I still saw her as weak.

Orla feels my judgment of the many parts of her personality that I most certainly love and wouldn't change if I were more patient and could release my own anxieties about the world. Together, Orla and Mum are teaching me that I need to focus less on the world and more on trusting her ability to navigate it, and that just like Mum, her softness in no way diminishes her strength. Orla is excellent at articulating her feelings and, as she grows, is developing a beautiful ability to advocate for herself, a skill Mum also developed out of necessity over the years. Yet too often, my response toward them doing so has been an exasperated and superior tone of voice, which ironically, is similar to the one I heard and felt from Dad about Mum, and, to a lesser degree, myself, when I was a child and a teenager. I don't judge Dad for that. I empathise with him as I now understand where that may have come from, but I use this reflection to help me take a different direction.

I don't believe I would have matured enough to get this level of insight before it was "too late" in Orla's life, had it not been for Mum's death. I have learnt so much about myself through parenting, but these lessons come through insight from my "daughtering", and I'm not sure if I would have looked in that direction otherwise.

I often felt like Mum "demanded" me to access and reflect on deep parts of myself I was not motivated to look at. I found that draining, yet now her wisdom is evident. I'm sure she is extremely proud of me and is sharing my relief that it is still possible to steer my relationship with Orla, and, for different reasons, Arlyn, onto a path where my girls have no doubt of my admiration, not just adoration, of them, let alone to an outcome where I can be proud both in the moment and in the future of my mothering; the role I value most of all.

My new identity as both a motherless daughter and a mother to teenagers has coincided, but rather than focusing on the loss of Mum at such a critical time in my life, I chose to see it as providing me with so many crucial extra learning opportunities. Even if it fluctuates depending on the day, I can make peace with her not being here to help and guide me because her life and her death continue to shape who I am. When I see it like that, the girls, Mum, and I all benefit.

When Sam and I were growing up, it appeared that I was more like Dad, and he took after Mum. Sam had Mum's fair skin; he was a very vague, little thing. He was gentle and had a much more easy-going nature. I was much more intense, had a sharper wit and, as the oldest, exerted my dominance. That shifted as we grew, but the changes became more obvious once we were in our 20s.

I started to look more like Mum while Sam morphed into looking like Dad and became more focused, more extroverted, and with that, a leader in his workplace and social life. I remained the ambivert that I have always been, but became more introspective and analytical, and having children really accelerated that. At the time of Mum's death, Sam and I were a mixture of our parents and in many ways still are, but as the years progress, I am increasingly becoming more like her. She'd love that I'm reading more often and the genre of books I'm choosing. She would be delighted that I'm writing this book! She would be so very happy, not only because it gives me allocated time to spend with her, grieve, and reflect, but as a writer, she would love that I am doing something creative and sharing her passion.

As much as I am benefiting from and enjoying the writing process, when it comes to reliving how deeply irritated I often used to feel about her, I am hating it. It was easier to write about her last breath than it was to reflect on how often I treated her as though she was a pain in my arse.

I want to be honest, and I know doing so serves a positive purpose, but it makes me physically agitated to acknowledge it. The strength of the sadness in the "new death bubble" brought with it a subconscious relief because it distracted me from how burdened I used to feel by her doing nothing other than being her. But the journey of grief has directed me back to reality, and I can't and shouldn't avoid it. I am still working on this "module", unravelling it, taking ownership, but trusting that with her help, the bullshit that infiltrated the beautiful aspect of our relationship's complexity will be gone, and all that will be left is love.

So, as I grieve, our history is important. I need those stories, both magic and shit, to get me to that point. All the while, she watches on, enjoying guiding me on that ride while she waits patiently for me to get off and join her for a long, soft, tight, safe hug. Hopefully, she'll be at the bar, with a fancy cocktail for my efforts.

With all of this rambling on about "growth" and "clarity", I do wonder sometimes, *Have I really changed? Am I walking the walk, or just talking the talk?* I believe that fundamentally I have changed, but I could see and feel more evidence of it in the beginning.

I wonder if the powers that control stress, habits, and routine are stronger than the magnificence of witnessing a death like the one that I did. As sad as it is to admit, I regularly find myself living life on autopilot. Even as I write this book where I so often refer to the blessings that being with Mum while she died offered me, I do not always live my life with intention and still take too many things for granted. It seems "in the real world", even magic can't overpower the requirements of day-to-day existence, where you don't just have yourself to consider and focus on. I am certainly crying and laughing with her less often and am less tuned into listening to her guidance, even though I expect her to provide it. Has life "poisoned" my ability to stay connected to her and the "new death" version of myself that I was enjoying?

The explanation isn't as simplistic as being part of the healing process because it feels more like regressing. I liked the feeling of vulnerability. I felt like I was a better, more patient, more grateful version of myself when my wounds were bleeding profusely. The hard grief that stops you in your tracks and continues to unfold layer after layer, even when you are successfully making it through each day, offered me so much clarity and connection to Mum. Rather than feeling like a progression once it eventually eased, that "milestone" was a hard one for me to adjust to. I guess nothing stays the same forever, and the real work of consciously engaging and putting into action the lessons that heavy grief provided begins as the bleeding subsides.

In the book *Dying to be Me*, although briefly, Anita mentions that even after such an intensely powerful experience, as the years passed, she often got caught up in the mixture of drama and monotony of life and was sometimes disconnected from living the life that she came back from death to live. My experience is very different, but I relate to the spark that death ignited in Anita's new life and was relieved to know that, even with the miracle she experienced, she had to remind herself to stay in the brightness of the light. Mum's death brought such intense perspective to my life. I was living authentically; my soul, the true essence of me, was leading the way. As painfully sad as I was, I was alive, I was loving, I was connecting.

As time progresses, I am realising that life brings both an ongoing challenge and an opportunity to step back into the light. Shadows caused by pain, loneliness, or even just routines are often cast over us for a purpose. Rather than getting bogged down with how I should be "doing it better" or maintaining a hardcore focus on the miracle of death to help me live my life "properly", I know the ebbs and flows of autopilot and awareness are there for a reason. Even though I sometimes lose focus, I have changed. I do have a different outlook now, and I am motivated to stay connected to the intensity of the light as I go forward into my new life without Mum here. She shines it on me so brightly that I can't ignore it for long.

Although nowhere near as powerful as an NDE, my exposure to death and what precedes it made me feel, in the earlier stages, like I had joined some special covert club. In those early months, I found myself wanting to talk about death all the time. I was almost desperate to find people whom I could relate to and was inspired to read about it, learn about it, and talk about it with anyone, in any context. I learnt that even referencing death is shocking to most people, like the unsuspecting man in Harvey Norman who asked who gave me the gift voucher I was using to buy a cocktail blender with. When I calmly but warmly responded, "My mum, just before she died", he nervously and quickly finished the transaction.

Aside from not agreeing with the taboo nature of the mere topic of death, I do, of course, understand and have empathy for those who need or prefer to keep it a "secret society". Death causes pain, and pain, understandably, isn't everyone's cup of tea. The varying avenues of gaining "admission to death club", mean the badge is one many would prefer to hurl into a fire rather than wear publicly. Although I, too, didn't ask for it, I value my membership in the possibly weird way that I do, and although I have calmed down a smidge, I do wish it didn't seem to be a case of "what happens in death club stays in death club".

If it were up to me, that would not be how we run things, not because I am happy, or "proud" that Mum is dead, but there is so much to be grateful for, because she also lived. I feel very lucky that I have been able to use something I had no control over and gave no permission to happen as motivation; that I am able to control the way I use the "death light beams" Mum shines on me brightly and consistently, to warm me with hope and help me to grow. Yet, it is evident that too much talking about death, perhaps it's particularly my experience with and approach to death, isn't something that most people are comfortable with.

I understand why it may seem strange that my response to Mum's death is so positive, but it's very isolating not feeling genuinely free to express myself, in case it is misinterpreted, or upsets someone. Talking about dying will, in most cases, bring Mum into the equation, which is part of my motivation, but the topic of death generally brings a level of depth to a conversation that I love. It can result in tears or laughter and enable you to truly connect and get to know a person much easier than talking about other topics that also do so, parenting, for example, where so much can get in the way of listening or speaking with clarity. Death just gets to the point nicely and quickly, and I find that I speak with less consideration for what people may think of me and listen without judgment. I could talk about the multifaceted topic of death and grief for hours, but alas, I can't. It's just not "the done thing", unlike crapping on about things like politics or health insurance. That's part of the reason for getting it out of my system via this book, I suppose!

It is such a big deal, unavoidable indirectly and directly, yet as was the case for me, it takes happening to someone we know, or it being put on our own horizon, before it's acknowledged to any real depth. We think of dying as being something physical, such as a lack of oxygen, heartbeat, and brainwaves. It's a "thought-ending" concept, rather than a thought-provoking one.

In our daily dealings, or even just through the news, we hear a massive variation of stories about it, how it happened, yet there seems to be so many boundaries around discussing it. Obviously, context and respect play a role, but generally, it is not something of mainstream interest. I know from experience that when it is brought into focus, even in a way that seems contextually socially acceptable, it isn't something that stays on the agenda long before people move on to what I consider to be "small talk" again.

When we do acknowledge it, we feel sorry for those left behind, or for the person themselves. We associate it with tragedy, but we don't seem to care about "death" in itself. We have empathy and an understanding of why a person would grieve, but not a common response or awareness that grief can be constructive, a tool of living, and that the relationship is ongoing. It seems to me that the words "death" and "grief" exclusively imply sadness. Likewise, generally, the emotion of grief is about *us. Our* loss and about being "left behind", rather than being inclusive of the now-dead person.

When grief results from death, it is always, at a minimum, a two-way street. I am sure that the change of approach is felt in both dimensions, and I believe that those who die grieve the loss of physical connection, too. I don't think they are totally immune to human concepts, but believe that after they "acclimatise", they only experience distress caused by watching their loved ones suffer. So, when or if we can take the focus off us, rather than conceptualising death and physical loss as the worst things that can ever happen to us and consider the possibility that things have improved for *them*, it helps the process for everyone. Grief can then shift and nestle itself forever into a place that fits more easily into the other parts of our daily lives. Regardless of the lifestyle, circumstances, and length of the life lived, my belief is that they are all radiating, *that they are love*, no longer human, which, whilst a gift, is also our biggest problem.

That may not be possible for everyone. I acknowledge that I am lucky to see it that way. But if we can get to a point where we mix our sadness (that we want to keep rather than *ever* be "healed" from) with the love we shared, and acknowledge the beauty, freedom, and joy they now experience independent of anything to do with us, instead of on what we have lost, grief can be easier to live with.

Prior to Mum's death, even a pessimistic person like me rarely focused on death. Fear of it happening and the impact of the loss, yes, but not death, as in the actual process and what happens short- and long-term afterwards, on both sides; here, and "there". Since Mum died, I have become a nut for it! I am so "into" death, it's so interesting, exciting even! It shifts concentration off me, where there's less to wonder about anyway, onto her, which allows me to hear her because I'm not dominating our "conversations" with my sorrow. I imagine her 'alive" in a place of depth. I feel peace for her. I am happy for *her*. I'm sure she misses us, but I know she is in a place she loves being, so my sadness and difficulties are more manageable.

Watching it happen was also something I'd never considered, other than fleeting thoughts that Mum would one day die, not what it would look or feel like after she did. I would never have imagined that her energy would get stronger. It would seem like I was exaggerating if I said how many times a day I think of her. Is that why I'm "healing" so quickly or "so well"? Rather than just enjoying the limelight, is she popping into my thoughts all day to help and reassure me that death is not a negative thing? That sure sounds like something she would do. Grief has ripped me open. It is teaching me so much about life, so to me, death isn't an entirely negative experience because grief has so much to offer. As it slowly transitions to integrate more into my life, I miss the intensity of it, but by maintaining a focus on death, rather than purely loss, my acceptance of physically losing her is a much easier path to navigate.

I have been aware right from the morning after Mum died that grief was also medicine. The dosage needed to be strong in those first days, weeks, and months. I was in a period of powerful grief, crying every day, sharing stories of Mum, saying her name all the time. It was hard, but a beautifully strange combination of being buried under a weight so heavy I could hardly blink, while also feeling like I could soar across the clear blue sky. I was more in tune with my grief in both an inward and outward way, often sharing a cuddle with my girls, particularly Orla, who would often sense my sadness and join me for a cry, or just mention that she was also missing Mimi. We would snuggle together in her bed at night and connect via our grief and our shared love of Mum.

During those times, Orla shared lots of stories of being gifted little signs from Mum. She was also slowly adjusting to life as a high schooler, and on many days during those first few weeks, she was escorted on her bike ride to school by four blue butterflies. We liked how there was a group of them; Orla figured it was Mum with Nanna, Dadda, and Uncle Michael. It makes sense that they would be together, keeping her safe. Blue butterflies would also show themselves to her on other occasions, flying away just as she thought to point them out, or a moment before anyone else arrived on the scene, making it clear they were only meant for her, making her feel very special (funnily enough, as common as I proposed butterflies are, I didn't see a single one that summer).

During one of our cuddling sessions, Orla told me how it helped her to imagine Mum was now a baby, born in Ireland around the time Mum died. A green-eyed baby with beautiful, reddish-golden locks of hair who would soon grow into a chubby toddler and have a wonderful, fresh start to life ahead of her. Those times with both of my girls, crying and laughing, were so precious because I was sharing my love of Mum and feeling *their* love for her, which brought joy to my heartache. I also got to experience what empathic little people they are, and how tuned into me they are, even when I wasn't outwardly displaying my pain.

It is evident to me that as I write this book, how I am "doing grief" is shifting, perhaps in part due to the intensive course of high-dose grief medicine administered through writing being so effective. I have set aside time almost every single week since starting to tell my story, our story, to record and be able to reflect now and in the future, on what I experienced, and the lessons offered and learnt.

Allowing myself time alone to honour my grief and my love for Mum, be creative and introspective, is such a gift. Although the physical space I have available to write in is not perfect, it is nevertheless comfortable. I have made it as much of a sanctuary as is possible. It is something I look forward to because of the writing process, but mainly because it's my time with Mum. A whole day together with no interruptions.

That said, it is absolutely full-on spending blocks of up to six hours, often forgetting to take a proper break, focusing on Mum, what I've lost, on my flaws, my growth, on our relationship. I have begun to feel as though I am grieving the grief itself. My response to 'Mum things", music, smells, and her actual belongings, has dulled, and without tears, the tangible connection I had with Mum isn't as readily available. I have come to terms with her death. Living life without her now sits within me. It's incorporated into my daily life and no longer sits beside me like a well-meaning but weird stranger who's trying too hard to get to know me but making me uncomfortable because I don't have reciprocal feelings.

Mum is dead.

Sometimes I still have to shake myself to resettle that inside me, but I know it, it's always there. That acknowledgment has shifted my grief from spurts of heavy crying, can't believe it, polished memories, to an everyday processing reality, which is an easier, less dramatic way to get through each day, but also a more mundane, resigned, or disconnected way of living and of connecting with her. It's a funny old thing. I am so dedicated to and enjoying writing this book, but it's also isolating me.

So, I just have to trust. Trust that, like the others, I will pass this module "moving through stale grief" and come out the other side able to enjoy the connection that the crying and sharing with others created and feel more of a pull to honour Mum outside of this process, instead of being so insular with my emotions. I hope to get to a point, albeit an updated version, where, for example, I can listen to a song that used to always set me off, and easily have a good, hard cry again.

To "remedy this problem", one day I listened to an audio of death rattles on YouTube in an attempt to be taken back to that time when my pain was so raw. A time before I had even considered what a life without Mum would be like, and was living with such an adrenaline of *feeling,* from a heart-directed space rather than so much cognition. That's an extreme and sicko thing to do, maybe I realise by the way, googling up "death rattle recordings". I felt weird doing it (imagine walking in to find some nutjob voluntarily listening to that sound!) but it was my attempt to reconnect with Mum, and with that version of myself too, I guess.

It was such a different kind of heartache in the hospital. I wasn't grieving, I wasn't up to that. The realisation that she was going to die is very different to the experience of her being dead. I could see her, touch her, and hear her, so hearing that horrific sound again helped me go back. I felt like I again had an audible connection with her, rather than relying on a telepathic one, which, despite being comforting, is never going to be as good.

Chapter 14 – Legacy

Mum, Jude, Sam's family and mine gathered at the end of the first lockdown period at Sam and Kel's house. Mum arranged the catch-up during lockdown on the phone with the kids, and in person once she could. They creatively called it the 'Out of Lockdown Party', and devised a theme – 'The Environment', meaning that the decorations had to be made from repurposed items. A menu was devised, and the kids made invitations and posted them between the households. I'll be honest, my initial response was that it was going to be yet another job for me, a pain in my arse to have to make the kids follow through on doing things Mum was encouraging them to do, when in reality their motivation was in theory only. It felt like more pressure from her to add to my workload, and it seemed unnecessary or over the top. Working through that, I realised I was missing a great opportunity to put into action the important lessons I had learnt during lockdown. I unravelled myself from my normal dismissive or belligerent attitude towards Mum's ideas and enjoyed the process and connection it offered as a part of the fun and meaningful occasion she envisaged.

The party was spent enjoying each other's physical company together for the first time in six months. We celebrated missed birthdays, Easter, and Mother's Day by swapping presents, cooking with and for each other and sharing time in our family way. With dinner done and the kids in bed, Sam, Mum, and I sat on the deck drinking and chatting, and Mum started talking about Mother's

Day, a day she had never been a fan of. It was a day she felt she was being slotted into rather than genuinely appreciated. She had spent many Mother's Days when we were kids, without us, or with us, but under a feeling of tension caused by the drama that Mother's Day always caused after my parents divorced. She had often spoken about wanting to claim the day back and heal the sadness it evoked in her. She wanted to acknowledge it in more of a real way, on a different date and make it a day less about expensive bunches of flowers (that we never bought for her anyway) and token gestures of "having" to get together, personalising it as our own way of celebrating motherhood in all its forms.

She spoke to us that night about her plan to finally act on creating this meaningful day. She wanted to take ownership of hosting it, regardless of the location it was held. She envisaged a new family tradition that would involve her spending time planning with the kids, encouraging her granddaughters to demonstrate respect and love for their mothers, their aunties of two generations, and her as the matriarch of their extended family, made up predominantly of women. She wanted to have fun collaborating with them on something they would easily engage with. As part of her healing, she suggested it be called Grandmother's Day, and the last weekend of each June was scheduled on our calendars. We talked about how it would be a day very similar to the 'Out of lockdown Party', where the kids set a theme and decorate the house accordingly. We would cook together and do a few set activities or games together, unlike our usual "tradition" of kids watching movies, adults getting on the turps.

During the early stages of planning Mum's funeral, Sam, Jude, and I decided that, considering it was the start of a new year, we would expand upon the funeral and dedicate the full year to celebrating Mum. We coined the phrase "Eilsfest", borrowing a concept Jude invented known as "Judefest", signifying the year she turned 50. Eilsfest would include such things as cleaning Mum's unit, so that instead of seeing that as just a traumatic task, we could see it as a means of not only honouring Mum together but also a way of spending time *with* her as we did so. Eilsfest would provide an opportunity to keep us connected and bring joy to our grief through ideas for how to spread her ashes or celebrate her birthday.

What better way of doing so than a dedicated weekend, a date already on the calendar that would enable us to get together in a special way that she would love. Here again, Mum's infinite wisdom is demonstrated. It was as though she had mapped it all out — die at a very convenient time of the year, check. Pick a funeral "theme" song, check. Make sure all of your things are organised and affairs are taken care of in a way that doesn't cause anyone stress or hassle, check. Mark out an annual date and develop an event that brings your loved ones together in a fun, easy, step-by-step way, which serves as a perfect memorial, check. So as "luck" would have it, the inaugural Grandmother's Day, perfectly positioned halfway through our first year without her, was one of the first big events on our Eilsfest calendar, ironically, possibly poetically, without Mum (in a physical sense at least).

The kids decided the theme should be 'Elephants on the beach at Sunset', yes, a pretty standard sort of party theme. Their reasoning was that they were three of Mimi's favourite things and the colours created by sunsets matched her vibe — pastel pinks and blues, yellow, peach, etc. They set about making artwork to decorate with and organising their party outfits to match the colour scheme. The weekend presented a good opportunity for the girls to go through Mum's trinket and scarf collections to choose what keepsakes they'd like. As planned, we played games together, such as a quiz guessing game with Mum's old family photos, an educational yet fun way for the girls to familiarise themselves with the wider family circle (Arlyn nailing it as the clear winner). Orla treated the girls to a pampering makeup session. Enjoying girlie time together like that was a fun and new way for them to interact and helped bridge the age gap between her and the others.

I spent many hours alone in the months between Mum dying and planning Grandmother's Day, trudging through Mum's massive amount of paperwork in preparation for a bonfire burn to kick off the weekend's celebrations. Over the course of many weeks, I smiled and cried my way through the good, the bad and the ugly of it all. I was relieved and a little bit surprised to find there were no skeletons. Mum had shared so much of what she had experienced and therefore, so much of her and what shaped her with me over the years. It was comforting to know that I knew her on that kind of intimate level, to that depth. Thankfully, there was also a lot to keep out of the "burn pile". Lots of creative writing, diary entries, letters and cards that were lovely to read and keep as evidence of Mum's existence and testimony to who she really was. The sheer amount of her life she documented was amazing, but no surprise, she was a writer after all. I felt both a sense of duty and a need to honour her, to honour myself, by reading every page. Such a massive gift, accelerating my grieving progression immensely. Perhaps it enabled me to get some 'credits" in my course and not even have to sit for some of the really difficult "modules" I may not have had the ability to pass otherwise.

The night before the inaugural Grandmothers Day, once the kids were occupied with their movie, we ventured outside into the winter night air, gathering around the fire pit to burn the things we didn't feel served a good purpose for anyone, including Mum, to keep. Court transcripts of the divorce and custody hearings, letters to and from her to toxic people she had endured, diary entries, medical and other records outlining the hardships, sad relationships and pain she lived through over the course of so many years. In amongst her extensively documented life, I had gathered several garbage bags full, so much paper that at times the mass of it threatened to extinguish the flames. But we kept it stoked while we enjoyed a drink, listened to music and reminisced. Cloud cover shifted across the sky, often revealing a full moon peeping through (the timing of which for such an occasion was a happy coincidence), until the last of Mum's heaviest sadnesses were no longer taking up space here on earth. None of that stuff matters to her anymore, and although it was part of who she was, so we neither want nor need to forget about it entirely, it was a profound experience for us to share the healing that Mum hoped to gain through Grandmother's Day through a cleansing fire. Emotionally, the content of some of those papers will remain with us to some extent, possibly forever, but physically eliminating it means we'll never have to relive that pain by reading about it ever again.

The first year without Mum also included our usual gathering for her birthday in October. Originally, it was going to be the piece de resistance of Eilsfest, with plans for a camping trip and ashes spreading ceremony, followed by an extended family gathering in a stunning rural area not far from where Mum was born. Sam and I had taken a road trip down there a few months after Mum's death to scope out a spot, which was another nice bonding experience facilitated by Eilsfest. None of this came to fruition because of border closures, which, whilst a big disappointment, in the grand scheme of Covid interfering with Mum's dying, was a small price to pay.

This meant her birthday lunch was a smaller gathering at the restaurant, we held her wake, and thankfully, it was another stunning day in the sunshine. We spent that night at Sam's listening to music, talking on the phone to Mum's three other sisters while a long slide show of photos of her we'd collated, played on repeat on the TV. When the time comes to scatter her ashes, we'll find another well-considered, meaningful and fun way to honour her. As has been the case with many things related to Mum's death, something good will come from something bad. For now, she still sits on our shelf getting the occasional chat while I dust around her dust and being acknowledged occasionally in other ways, like when the girls "dob" on me to her, for instance.

The lead-up to Christmas and the day itself were a lot harder than I imagined, made worse by an early Christmas morning phone call from Sam telling me he had Covid. He was the first case we knew of personally to have the virus. The news of his forced absence made me feel like the air had been sucked out of my lungs. Shaking and unable to cry properly from the pressure in my chest, I pulled myself together for the girl's sake, playing along as best as I could at my in-laws' breakfast gathering and enough to get through hosting the celebration at our house later that day. Although we had a nice enough time and a place for Mum was set at the table, I was unable to fully acknowledge her absence. It felt as though I was pretending that she wasn't being missed, which added to my sadness. Without Sam's support and his being there to offer my support to, on top of missing him in his own right on what is always a family day, I couldn't do it any other way without ruining the day for everyone, which would have made me feel worse.

The following week, a week before Mum's first anniversary, Covid continued to spread its wrath in the community, and the four of us tested positive. That was always going to be a hard week without that in the mix, so it felt like salt in my wounds. The girl's symptoms were quite mild, but it hit Ev and me hard. Christmas plans out of the way and only three weeks left before the start of term one, I had intended to kick off school holiday activities, but instead, we were stuck at home while most of our friends continued enjoying summer. Isolating was mentally draining and had none of the fun aspect of the "iso's" we'd done before in the knowledge that everyone else was doing so. The kids were irritated and so were very irritating to be with (a polite understatement). They were missing their friends, whom they hadn't seen for weeks and were, "fortunately", well enough to fight with each other constantly because of their frustration and boredom. That, as a backdrop to Ev and me spending the days and nights sweating and barely able to get out of bed, was exhausting. Empathising with why they were fighting, and them being miserable during their long-awaited summer holidays, was also upsetting. It was a fucking shit of a week, impacted in no small part by the impending anniversary.

Each day, January 9 grew closer, and I was reliving the countdown of events at the times they were unfolding one year earlier. The entire day and late into the night before she would have had her stroke was excruciating. Reliving everything was much worse than I had anticipated because it caught me off guard. I had figured it would be about 'that day', not realising the lead-up would be so suffocating.

Watching the clock, conscious of exactly what I was doing that time last year, calling her about lunch, for example. I was fixating on what would have happened had I called her a day or two earlier when I originally thought to, or if she was hearing my calls. Sam phoning to tell me what had happened; the first day with everyone in palliative care, the death rattle day. Each of those moments in time had so much happening within them now that I knew what was coming. I could dissect each "scene" individually, reliving the thoughts and feelings with the extra burden of the loss that I didn't understand then.

I was sick, cranky, tired, and so acutely aware of how much I had already and would always be missing Mum. Aside from an awareness that yet again, Covid's involvement in the story was manageable and therefore to be acknowledged as a blessing (at least we didn't have it then), I experienced none of the laughter, camaraderie and magic of those days one year ago and in the weeks after. Some of my favourite times, now juxtaposed one year on, as certainly not. The "in real time" experience of those days in the hospital seemed "easy" by comparison. Now, there was no Sam. No Jude. No Mum. Just sorrow, constant breathless tension in my chest and deep despair. It was a hell of a week.

Our "iso" period was over just in time for the anniversary date (thanks, Mum, that helped shake off some of my misery). Ev, the girls and I started the day with a picnic breakfast only to have it cut short due to a deluge of rain. Later that morning, I caught the train to meet Sam, and we dropped off a thank-you card and flowers at the palliative care unit. Due to the increasing influx of COVID, we were only able to leave it at the front door. I would have loved the opportunity to give it to Mum's nurses and, if possible, spend some time sitting in the garden. I had a desperate urge to go back there. It was a place of such intensity, so perhaps some might say strangely, I really wanted to immerse myself back into those memories and feelings, despite at times being so impatient to get out of there a year earlier. Aside from it being the last place I'd been with Mum, it was a sacred place where we'd all connected on such a deep and authentic level and shared something beautiful. I'd missed being in that room, I guess. A haven in hell.

Lisa Birrnie, in her book *A Good Day to Die*, has collated a variety of 'death stories' in connection to a palliative care unit in Melbourne where she spent time specifically studying the merits and flaws of euthanasia. Regardless of the inspiration for her research and in some ways as a direct result of it, it is a fantastic book that provides so much insight into people, spirituality, death and end-of-life care. When done correctly, she depicts the palliative care setting as being one of decency and respect. A mutually transforming place of intense authenticity and healing. Despite my short stay, I deeply relate to that. Experiencing death from the vantage point of a daughter who was encouraged to have the confidence and therefore the ability to co-direct the experience where possible, is obviously very different to what it would be like working there, but I can easily imagine the impact being in that environment on a daily basis would create. The profound relationships the workers must develop with people going through loss of life, or of a loved one, without the need for a shared history and in many cases, because there is not one.

As discussed in Lisa's book, the very nature of that environment not only gave us permission but *encouraged* our feelings to exist on a higher level than any concept related to logical reason. We took charge of our experience; we would have fought to do so if it had been necessary, but thankfully, we were given the space and support to do so. It was such a powerful way to exist, even if it was only for three days. It was there that I really tuned into what I have, rather than what I don't. I wasn't foreseeing the future, strangely, not once. I was completely focused on Mum, as she was, not as she had been, or what was ahead. I felt immersed in the pure unconditional love we shared.

Having spent time in both comparative ends of the spectrum, in my experience, it was a much more powerful place than a maternity ward. While, of course, the physical acts of labouring and giving birth are miracles, from my perspective, the beginning of the continuum was in many ways psychologically harder. There's so much expectation and anticipation at the start, not that it's necessarily a negative thing, but you do feel those pressures. You have no guarantee of what the outcome will be. You do have a clear reference point of what you imagine and hope will eventuate, but for the most part, thoughts dominate feelings. You experience hope in palliative care, too, but in any case, where death is the focus, all conditions are off the table. In essence, it's simplified; you know the outcome. It is death. Control and with it, pressure, is therefore lessened as feelings dominate thoughts. You have no choice but to be in the moment.

I acknowledge it's not always a positive experience. Many people suffer their darkest times, dying and caring for loved ones who are, it can also be horrific, but the book offers a perspective from someone who worked with palliative people as being "like glancing into paradise", which I can relate to. I try to hold on to that feeling. It helps me, brings me gratitude and comfort. When I take myself back to being with Mum as she died, I feel connected to something "bigger" that offers me a bird's eye view of myself and directs me away from trivial shit I may have otherwise perceived as important and towards the light of the life I want.

After dropping off the flowers, Sam and I went to lunch again at our restaurant by the sea, something I had been really looking forward to after not seeing him on Christmas Day. After asking Mum all year, she had *finally* gotten her act together and found Sam a new job, but unfortunately, he was rostered to be on call that weekend. Throughout lunch, he was constantly on the phone with issues that couldn't be ignored. Being sick all week, then rain at the picnic, rushing with the flowers and the distractions at lunch, was all capped off by Sam having to hurry through lunch, then he had to leave early to go to work, rather than spending the day together as planned. We got caught in traffic as he took me to the station, and despite running to the platform, I missed my train mere by seconds, so had to wait an hour for the next one, in unseasonably freezing cold wind and rain. A hell of a week, followed by a shit of a day. I didn't feel like the anniversary had been about Mum at all. It had just been a series of one distracted, annoying or disappointing episode after the other. Given my state of mind and heavy heart in the lead-up, it was hard to hold myself together in public as I eventually made my way home.

The day before this shittiest of days, Mum reminded me of a movie suggestion she'd once made that she thought the girls would enjoy watching with Ev and me. I knew it was her talking to me because, totally unrelated to anything I was doing, that memory popped into my mind. Home and showered, I was focusing on preparing myself emotionally for the next day (aware it would be the first day of my second year without her), when she nudged me to remind me again. It happened to be a perfect time of the night to start a movie, so I scrolled and scrolled through messages from Mum before finally finding the name of it. The girls were excited by the idea of watching a movie with us, it's not a normal occurrence in our household (after all, when they watch movies, we get on the turps), so with a happy school holidays lack of routine vibe, we grabbed some popcorn and made ourselves comfy on the lounge, having no idea of the movies premise but just trusting in Mum's / Mimi's recommendation. We knew it must have something to do with *What We Did On Our Holiday* as suggested by the title and that it starred Billy Connolly, so I knew I would love it based on that alone, but was intrigued how it would be suitable for the kids, Mum's text assuring me that swearing wasn't an issue.

What followed was the happiest couple of hours I had had in weeks. The movie was a goodie, regardless of the timing of us watching it on Mum's anniversary, "just by chance", being perfect, I highly recommend it, but among so many other instances where "timing is everything", this was certainly one. It could not have been more spot on, on so many levels, shockingly so! It signified an end to that tough fortnight and reminded me to count my blessings and laugh again. I was so grateful to my old mate Billy and my old mate Mum. She capped off that year for me in her usual style by offering wisdom and humour.

I had done it. I had survived the first year of my life without Mum! Like the profound feeling I had, staring at

Orla on her first birthday, I felt a strangely similar feeling of achievement. A big milestone, one that will never be experienced ever again. The first year of being a mother. The first year without a mother. In both instances, I had gone through the most accelerated growth I have ever experienced. Not only had I made it, but I was ready now to keep going forward into the unknown of all that lies ahead. Ready to keep growing and keep learning how to be the best mother to my daughters and the best motherless daughter I can be to myself. Fortunately, gracefully, joyfully, patiently, but willingly, waiting for the whistle.

Epilogue

The experience of writing this book, which I started seven months after Mum's death, has taken me down so many paths during the four-ish years it took from start to finish (with quite a few rewrites). Milestones like her funeral, birthdays, Christmases, anniversaries of her death, Grandmother's Days, and ashes spreading celebrations, mixed with ordinary moments, like housework days without Mum on the phone. Life is going on. I have changed so much during that time, evidenced by this record of my responses, thoughts, and lessons learnt along the way. These twists and turns, starting with powerful, "normal", "fresh" grief, then surfacing in the second year, where I did quite well, have now moved to intense inner loneliness and a "settled" realisation that I have lost my one and only ever true person to share my whole self with.

There are things about me, things I've done or thoughts I have, that nobody knows, not one person. A select few of these things I could make peace with sharing with someone if the context called for it, Jude perhaps, but everything I've done, every thought that causes me pride, insecurity, or internal shame, I know I could share with Mum; I wouldn't need to pick and choose which ones. Despite knowing that Jude wouldn't judge me, I couldn't and wouldn't open that sacred space with her, or anyone else. No one else can fill that void. Those secrets of my soul, now a sad space, is only for her. That depth of me is only for her.

Her love for me makes love feel like a stupidly ordinary, inadequate word. I feel how deep it is through feeling it for my girls. I love them deeper than they love me. She loved me deeper than I loved her, and there is nothing that compares to knowing you are loved like that. As a woman, and compounding that, as a mother, grieving her is a very dark hole to constantly have to jump over. I *need* to share with her. I have so much more understanding of "us" now that my girls are where they are in their lives. I am "back" to the beginning of how heavy it was when she died in many ways, but because life has moved on, this new version of grief is harsher, because it's quieter.

It is so integrated into my life that I now experience everyday life through it. I desperately miss her. I miss things I didn't know I noticed when she was alive. I miss how she used to pick up crumbs on her fingers and absentmindedly eat them as she talked. I miss the smell of her car. I miss the way she folded plastic bags to store them neatly. I miss how she used to violently scratch her ear canal. I miss the obvious things. I miss her loving and proud looks at me while I interact in a group. I miss the softness of her skin. I miss knowing glances at each other that cause hysterical laughter without a word spoken. I miss her voice. Her face. Her advice.

That being said, I have arrived at this point today, the fourth anniversary of that life-transforming day, with a visual image of myself as having much wider eyes and a physical feeling of having a gentler heart. In that image is also the invisible umbilical cord that Mum used to describe in such detail to Sam and me when she moved out after Dad and her split up, and continued to reference in the years that followed. A beautiful string, whatever colour we chose for however we were feeling. The same string that has always connected us, Sam and I, have never existed without it.

Cutting it at our births just changed its form, turning it invisible, but it never disappeared; it never stops performing its magic. Via that cord, we are forever connected to the life source. Mum is my life *source*, and her death has created a new life *force* within me. Blessed by her through life and death, I go forward with wide eyes, a softer heart and a pretty, shimmering rainbow-coloured string connecting me to her forever. Just as she promised.

Acknowledgements

Thank you, Mum, for sharing your love of language, encouraging me to have a wide vocabulary, and teaching me the importance of using my written and spoken words wisely (yes, "words are weapons", but, as you also know, they can be bandages).

Thank you for the idea of writing this book (I'll give you that credit, even though I'm not entirely sure if it was you or me) and for helping me with words or structure when I got stuck. The book is dedicated to Ev and the girls, Sam and Jude, but it was written *for* you, Mum. Thank you for your unwavering belief in me. Thank you for loving me to the deepest depths of your physical and invisible versions. Thank you for my heart, both in rose quartz and beating inside me forms. I will use both wisely to carry me through and make you proud. I'm so lucky to be yours. You did such a good job, Mum.

P.S. — You're published!!!

Thank you, universe, for this book taking me wherever it is that it will take me. I trust implicitly that you know the way...

To every single one of my family and friends (who knew I was writing this book) who gave me encouragement and cheered me on. You all seemed so effortlessly, genuinely confident in my ability, which was both daunting and humbling. Thank you for asking for updates, for never doubting me. Your kindness has meant so much. Knowing you were all there "beside me" inspired me and made this very solitary process feel less lonely and therefore less overwhelming. You are part of the reason I kept going and eventually finished. Thank you from the cockles of my little heart.

A big nod to the McCabe whistle. What an ingenious and effective method of communicating — it makes me wonder why whistling is usually reserved for getting the attention of dogs. Our lovely little sing song "Where are you?", or the faster "Get here now" whistle, has always been a part of my life. I look forward to hearing it when my own time comes, and watching it being used by many more McCabe generations.

To Earl Grey tea (thanks, Trish!), hazelnut coffee (thanks, Jude!), falafel wraps, and smoked tuna with rocket, pine nuts, parmesan, and balsamic dressing salad. To my fluffy pink blanket (thanks, Mum!), my writing shirt (thanks, Meg), incense, my balancing balm (thanks, Kel), rainy days, sunshiney days, and peace-and-quiet alone time. To all the "death books" (thanks, Jude). To the background tunes that often made their way into my foreground while I wrote, and music in general, but of that first year in particular, **I could not have done it without the music**.

To Dad. I'm not likely to write another book for you, I'm sorry to say. Mum got in first, and I'm not sure I've got a sequel in me. Book or no book, know that I am so grateful for your love and support and all the help you give us with the girls (including our fluffy, youngest one). It's been great having you just down the road, being able to catch up for our little cuppas and lunches. I am so lucky to have you. You're not a bad old codger. I really love you, Dad.

To the palliative care team of early January 2021. You guys turned our shithouse situation into a gift. I am forever so grateful that all four of us landed in your care.

To Maree, Clint (Heartfelt Funerals), and Jo (Big Love Ceremonies). You are all so good at your jobs! So genuine, warm, and reasonably priced! Thank you for making us feel so well cared for, for making us and Mum, feel so special. We felt like we were the only people you were dealing with, like nothing was too much trouble. We all still talk about the three of you and will forever appreciate you helping us send Mum off so perfectly.

To all the "daughters of now 'unseen' mothers" out there, especially Mel, Tan, Aunty Anne, Aunty Chellie, Aunty Debra, my BS, Aunty Raema, Yvonne, Julie, Nicole R, Trish, Karen, Nicole H, Jo, Sarannah, and Danielle. To mother-in-lawless Kel. She really loved you, Kel.

To my cousins in our McCabe sing-along messenger group. So "us", to turn something that was something, into a completely different tangent. You have no idea how much you helped me through those first few months after Mum died. Being able to share my songs and thoughts was such an important coping strategy for me. I love you all.

Dearest Jacinta, may the beauty of your Jossygirl's sunflower light, shine through to reach you in your darkness, directing you forward and eventually, upwards, when you see her beautiful, big, blue eyes smiling at you again.

To Helen. We barely knew each other, but apparently, that is irrelevant. You had a profound impact on me long before I ever considered myself as one day being a motherless daughter. Through you, I was faced with imagining my girls in that position. That changed the way I mother them to this day, and forever more. That vantage point turned your curse into my blessing. My sobbing despair on graduation day could not be contained. Watching your little love on that stage ripped my heart to shreds. I still think of you from time to time when I chop the veggies for dinner.

To Motherless Daughters Australia. The existence of your organisation — the unknown-to-you connection and support I received via your Facebook group — helped me so much in those earlier days. The champa's cheers to all the mums at the high tea I attended in that first year without Mum was a pivotal moment for me, and despite possibly cracking too many jokes for the occasion, I felt very supported in that space. Danielle and Eloise, you should be so proud of the work you do. Without a doubt, your mums certainly are.

To my proofreading team, Ning and Katherine. Thank you for taking the time to help a stranger. I value and appreciate your input and support. Thank you so much to Trish for teeing that up, and my deepest appreciation for taking on the role as my editor. Your time, effort, and skillset kick-started me again when I felt like I had run out of petrol, enabling me to proceed with the process. Your friendship truly went above and beyond.

Thanks to Jenny for your time and suggestions, and a huge thanks to Fiona and her team at InHouse Publishing for finalising the edit and *finally* getting me on track with the actual publication — *finally!* A big thank you for the assistance with my cover art to Cara, and again, to Fiona from InHouse Publishing for the final artwork, design, and formatting. I sincerely appreciate your understanding, patience, ideas, and talent. It's surreal to hold a dream in your hands, see it, feel it, and share it. Thank you to everyone who contributed to making that happen.

Thank *you* if you have read this little self-published book of mine (and Mum's). We sincerely appreciate it. Please post a review online or let other people know about it by good ol' word of mouth if you have enjoyed it (and just say nothing if not, but really, why have you read this far?)

This death and writing thing is a real passion for me, and this process has stretched me far beyond my comfort zone, but I'd love to see if it can take me somewhere. If you feel you can help me in any way with that, I'd be very grateful.

Cheers!

Keep it real,

Lynda

Bibliography

BBC Films Creative Scotland. (2014). *What We Did on Our Holiday* [Film]. United Kingdom.

Birnie, L. H. (1998). *A Good Day to Die*. Text Publishing Co.

Moorjani, A. (2015). *Dying to Be Me: My Journey from Cancer, to Near Death, to True Healing*. Hay House.

January 4ᵗʰ 2021

Our family gathered for Christmas at Sam and Kelly's place this year. Ralph was there, and Jude, of course. Sam's good mate Brock and his family joined us for a drink and a jump on the tramp before dinner. We spent the afternoon shaded by a tarp that Sam had rigged up in the backyard, eating from festive platters, drinking delicious cocktails, laughing, and feeling relaxed in the warm rays of the late summer afternoon. Sam and Kel always do a great job of hosting. They work very well together when it comes to many things, and entertaining guests is one of them. A good time was had by all, with a beautiful meal and some drunken sing-along shenanigans, so a very Merry Christmas it was indeed.

I returned home on Boxing Day, spending the remainder of that day and the lead-up to the New Year resting and recovering from the noisy hustle and bustle of the celebrations.

It was another quiet weekend, the first of the year. I spent some time reflecting on the year that was, thinking about the new year that would inevitably be filled with change. Each year brings change, regardless of how seemingly insignificant or mundane, energising, or even frustrating. Sometimes it's an intense squall, sometimes a subtle breeze, but regardless, the winds of change blow the pages of our lives to keep unfolding. Although at times I have felt powerless against the direction it takes me, or that the air had stagnated, I am aware that I am always experiencing and benefiting from change and that it is indeed always all around me. Change of any kind allows me to keep gathering knowledge, keep going and especially when I feel like I'd like to stop, I know a change will come. This will be the year I will move on from my home of the past decade, so the gusts will be stronger this year. I am hopeful that they will blow me in a positive direction rather than having to encounter the exhausting headwinds I seem to so often come up against.

I received a call from Orla on New Year's Day. It was lovely to hear her sweet little voice. Imagining her saving my name into her mobile phone and making that call is another reminder that transformation is indeed all around. Even in such a simple thing as getting a phone call from your granddaughter on her first mobile phone, the first call she had made to anyone on it, signifies one of the changes that this year, 2021, will bring. A year where my first grandchild goes to high school while my last one starts school, and the years of caring for my grandchildren while their parents go to work are no longer required. What changes will that bring to my role as their grandmother, I wonder?

I phoned Anne on Saturday to wish her a happy birthday on Sunday and spent the remainder of the day on the phone with Mary. I enjoy hearing her stories about her little grandsons. It's lovely to be able to share experiences with her now that she's a grandmother. By the sounds of it, she's very settled and revelling in that important role. It'll be Michael's birthday on the 5th. I miss him deeply, but I know he hasn't gone far. I'll take some time to spend with him on Tuesday, as I always do, for what should have been his 63rd year.

I feel more empowered this year than I have for a while. I'm finally feeling the possibility that I am not as stuck as I have felt I have been. I am on the verge of a shift, and a positive change for me, separate from the impact that changes in other people's lives have upon me. This is *my* time. I do catch myself feeling unsure, jaded, and nervous, but I have to remain open, trusting, and patient, as always. Such a heavy, contrasting way to always be pulling myself through life, but maybe that in itself will begin to shift for me this year. I've been enjoying the slower pace that comes when Christmas has been and gone. No planning or shopping for presents, the busy lead-up is replaced by enjoying the warm weather and taking time to set my intentions for what lies ahead.

In the short term, I'll need to get some groceries, so I might do up a list and get myself organised to get out to the shops this morning before my phone appointment with the doctor after midday. I plan to continue my research this afternoon. I'm not really sure where I'm up to with some of it. I think I've got some tidying up to do with the Whitmores', and I intend on spending some time over the next few days organising and perhaps finalising some of the documentation I have for Erin, if my energy allows. We have not been in touch to have a proper chat about things since her text in November, which I am a bit frustrated about, but I do understand that she is much busier than I am.

I'm hopeful that this new year will bring about some positive developments with regard to our collaboration, as it was something that energised me and created a feeling of optimism when we initially discussed it. It's something meaningful to look forward to and will also take a bit of a load off my shoulders to be working with someone, another change for this coming year. I'm curious to know what information she has gathered over the years. It'll be interesting to see how we work together as researchers, and I'm looking forward to developing our relationship as a happy byproduct of that process.

Thankfully, I wasn't long at the shops and wasn't rushing to get home for my telehealth appointment. Dr Suleman seems to think I should stay with the dosage I'm on, for the time being at least, so now, once I get these groceries away, I'll make myself a bite to eat, then follow through with my research plans. Then I might see if I can make it out for a little stroll along the water before dusk, if I'm feeling up to it, and if the esplanade doesn't look too crowded.

***

Michael is here, although I am not sure where here is. I am aware of a tight sensation in my chest, but I do not feel pain. I have a memory of experiencing intense pain, exhaustion, dehydration, and desperation, although I am not sure if that is a recent memory, one from a long time ago, or sometime in between. But Michael is here, so I am not concerned with figuring that out. For now, I can only feel the peaceful love of Michael. Michael, my beautiful baby brother, my kind, curious, and easy-to-be-with brother, Michael, is here.

I am not focused on how, why, or on anything other than allowing his presence to fill me because his being here is all that matters. I have missed him so desperately, and now, he is here! I have yearned for him for so long. He is saying happy birthday, and it feels as though he is taking me somewhere, but we don't seem to be anywhere, or moving; we are just *here*, together. I'm not questioning where or when or how we will get there, or whose birthday it is, for that matter. There is no need to know anything or to rush. Michael doesn't rush me.

Michael is here! Michael is here!

The winds of change have blown Michael my way!

All I feel is Love. Peace. Acceptance.

Love.

Love.

Warm, deep, genuine love.

I am Love.

Mothers of The Clan

Eileen McCabe©
October 2009

For my sisters.
Dedicated to the parents and brother we all love and share.

The cause for tears is over now; the
cycle is complete.
It's time to gather diamonds that are
scattered at our feet.
To build the family fires again and
make our kids a home,
For lost or weary souls to rest, to
guide them when they roam.
Hear the Old Ones call you as they
pound the drums of Time.
Feel your heartbeat echo as they
shout out, "You are mine!"
"So come on, Ann, stand staunch with
Chell; the young rely on you.
Hurry, Eil, take Debbie's hand and
Jude, you're in this too."
"The family was our sacred toil; we
left it in your care.
We trust you *all* to care for it, now
we're no longer there."
"This September needs you *five*
Mothers, to tend places of the heart.
So babes unborn will know through
time where they each had their start."
"Remember you are sisters, girls, in
all you do and say.
Deep courage finds forgiveness; with
true love to lead the way."
"Old vines that set our family tree,
watch o'er you matriarchs,
So get together, 'have your say', but

listen with your hearts."
"*All* families have their customs that
tell souls how they belong.
So sometimes meet, to laugh and cry,
and sing old family songs."
"From kinship's fire ancestors rise, as
phoenix bird of old.
And we will come to listen, when our
yarns once more are told."
"With sorrows ash now washed by
tears, 'you have your jobs to do.
We left you firm foundations, so
hearth fires can burn anew."
"Always stick together, girls; 'be loyal'
to your bond.
Show the young who come behind,
our legacy lives on."

My sisters, now I turn to you to ask
how you respond!
Will we stand proud together when
we meet them o'er beyond?
Our turn has come to take their place;
lead wisely for the young.
United, we all feel the same; we *know*
that we are one.
Each one a precious crystal flame
that makes our family shine.
That burns the light of heritage, so
worthy and Divine.
As Marnie, Darma, Mimi, Muma,
Aunty, resolute.
Each Elder is our family's heart with
love that's absolute.

Listen to the Wind, Baby

Written by Eileen McCabe, July 2010, and Lynda Ryan and
Eileen McCabe, 10th September 2021

Listen to the wind, baby, listen to the wind.
Hear the voices call your name? Listen to the wind.

**Wild angels dance a crazy dance to join you in your
game.
Listen, baby; listen to them calling out your name.
As jingle jangle branches dance, you laugh in sheer
delight.
And little mouth so wide with glee, squeal with all your
might.**

Listen to the wind, baby, listen to the wind.
Hear as voices call your name. Listen to the wind.

**Do the old ones tell you that they watch you as you grow?
Do they whisper secret things that only they would know?
They whistle loudly, calling to you through the untamed
storm.
Orla, Orla, peek a boo, on this windy morn.**

Listen to the wind, baby, listen to the wind.
Hear the voices call your name. Listen to the wind.

**They watch you taking hold of life and make it all your
own.
Your special brand of magic will remind the folks of
home.
Can you hear them, baby girl, as you now sit and stare?
As gentle breezes kiss your nose and rumple up your
hair?
Reaching out with tiny hands to touch their unseen faces.
You stretch your little arms out wide, accepting all their
Graces.**

Listen to the wind, baby, listen to the wind.
Hear the voices singing to you? Listen to the wind.

Hear the voices call your name, all dancing on the wind.
Each day a new adventure; such wonders will it bring.
It rushes up the valley, and it rattles through the trees.
Feel their love caress you as it's carried on the breeze.
Feel them kiss your rosy cheeks, listen to what they say.
Orla Shae, Orla Shae, we have come to play.

Listen to the wind, baby, listen to the wind.
Angels' wings are on the air, so listen to them sing.

Now it's time to wave goodbye, so hear their wild refrain.
But they will come another day, and you will play again.
The wind will whistle pretty tunes to carry you away.
They'll carry you to Slumberland until another day.
So, close your eyes, my little one and softly will they sing.
New adventures filled with love, tomorrow they will bring.
They croon to you a lullaby, through windowpane they peep.
So, close your weary little eyes, as now it's time to sleep.

There's our baby! We see you!
So, listen to the wind.
Orla, Orla, we see you.
Listen to the wind.

To Lewis

Eileen McCabe©
April 2008

Little one who never was,
it's time to say goodbye.
Our hearts were stirred by heaven's kiss;
on angels' wings you fly.
We loved you from the very start,
but still, you couldn't stay.
Your life was but a dream for us,
and now you go away.
Your mummy cries, your daddy sighs,
but they both understand.
You could not stay, but when someday,
they hold a tiny hand.
They'll feel the gift you gave to them;
they'll know you through that love.
As they embrace their babe-in-arms,
you'll watch them from above.
Little one who never was,
it's time to let you go.
Our family is much richer for
the grace you came to show.
Though time may bring me other babes
to hug and help me smile.
I know that angels hold my heart,
through you, my *first* grandchild.

My Mother's Hands

Eileen McCabe©
2008

At the end of my mother's life, I sit by her bed as she sleeps, watching her hands. They lie there, one crossed over the other, so soft, fair, and quiet. Each elegantly elongated nail is painstakingly painted in a soft pearl pink, a colour we, her five daughters, have come to associate with her as she has grown older. Her skin is pale and soft, and her fingers are dainty and delicate. These look to be the hands of a lady.

It could be supposed that they have never been exposed to hard toil, spending all their time in pursuits of the idle. This is far from the case, however. These little hands have been busy, very busy, through the years. They have washed other people's clothes and scrubbed their floors. They have cooked meals, mended clothes, created, and done a lot of work in their existence.

These hands have milked cows, caressed the feverish head of a child, gripped tight the hand of a young one learning to negotiate the traffic, and brushed away the hair from the forehead of a man as he lay dying beside her. These hands have earned their rest, their pampering and preening.

Such busy hands.

Such productive hands.

Creating memories hands...

Prelude:

Annie

Eileen McCabe©
2017–2018

Time fades as memories gather, soft as shadows in the twilight. Gentle phantoms rally to soothe her restless soul. These friendly ghosts surround her to ease an endless ache for loved ones who now "sleep" beneath the sod. A dream-weave web of yesterdays, enfolds her lonesome spirit, protecting it from the bleak reality of this place of pitiless charity, where succour is dispensed through demeaning, detached indifference. Worn and hungry, her heart flees to other seasons; other spaces, where life is full and matters.

There, folks know her name, so she is no longer alone, but among her long-gone dear ones. They extend their welcome and take delight in her presence. In this secret world of precious memories, she is no longer unwanted and forgotten in the evening of her life. She is Home.

A vast disparity exists between these hidden corners of her mind and the place she now finds herself. Here, she resides among strangers who ignore and neglect her. The workers attend to her basic physical needs with cold-hearted efficiency. They care nothing for her yearnings. Her compliance with their will is their only concern. They believe that emotional comfort is unnecessary for an ancient one who has outlived her usefulness. A head befuddled with rubbish requires no regard, so no consideration is required. Lacking insight, overworked and, in some cases, just plain heartless, no thought is spared to where her tired old mind takes shelter.

Unbeknownst to them, she has left the pointless existence they have enforced on her. Enfolded in the safety of her "yesterdays", Old Annie is with her people once again!

Mrs Magee

Eileen McCabe©
2017–2018

She needed a refuge from the hard going that life had become. They told her she would be taken in, but she still felt unsure. Those places had a bad reputation, like the old workhouses, some said. But what other choice was there? She had nowhere else to go.

Mrs Ann MAGEE (known as Annie[1]) stood no more than 4'10" (147 centimetres). Despite her small stature, the old Irishwoman was normally fiercely independent, but unhappy events had taken that away, forcing her to seek help. She had travelled well over 530 miles (around 860 kilometres) to get this far, in Queensland's sweltering summer sun. She waited on the dock to be told when it was time to embark, so the final leg of that arduous journey could begin. Heading to a place she could only hope would become her new home.

Preparation for the regular run across Queensland's Moreton Bay was a well-practised drill for the captain and crew of the Otter, berthed at the Kangaroo Point wharf. On Tuesday morning, 29 January 1901, they went about the business of loading the old steam clipper with a minimum of fuss. Supplies for the prison on St. Helena were stowed appropriately to be dropped off first. The ferry would then turn south to the Peel Island Lazaret, before heading across to North Stradbroke Island to deliver the last of supplies and passengers to the old docks at the Dunwich Benevolent Asylum.

Right on time, they got underway. With Annie and the other passengers safely on board, the boat pulled away from its moorings before turning east toward the mouth of the Brisbane River and the open waters beyond. The most challenging part of the voyage was always the treacherously shifting sand bars at the river mouth, but once the captain negotiated the ancient vessel past that point, it was usually an easy cruise across the sheltered waters of the lagoonal bay.

Annie had been a widow for a long time. She had only been in Queensland since 1897, arriving with her youngest daughter Elizabeth,[2] son-in-law Frank,[3] and their three youngest children.[4] They came from the Bourke district of New South Wales, with the likely plan being to put bad times behind them and make a fresh start on the Queensland side.[5]

It is not hard to imagine that the birth of a healthy baby boy before the year was through would be seen as a sign that good luck was with the family and their lives were changing for the better.[6] Such a strong start to their bright new beginning would surely have given them cause to celebrate. Regrettably, their joy was too short-lived.

By century's end, Lady Luck had turned her face, so her light no longer shone their way. Events of 1900 would bring more distress to this embattled family, rupturing kinship ties that had survived all the trouble and tribulation life had sent so far.

On reaching Queensland, they had gone straight to Cunnamulla as it was the ideal place to look for work. Two major stock routes converged there. A reliable watercourse made the area a convenient place to rest cattle coming from the north before turning them south towards the State border. The convenience of water was also the reason Cobb & Co set up their main western Queensland stopover there, which included substantial hotel accommodation. Other trades and businesses sprang up around it until all the infrastructure and convenience that could be expected in a thriving transit hub were there.

Annie and the ADAMS family remained there for about two years, but then relocated to Eulo, a small town about 45 miles (70 kilometres) to the west.[7] Sometime around 1900, Frank took his family 350 miles (560 kilometres) north, to Jundah in the Barcoo region of central western Queensland. Annie remained in Eulo. Why this change occurred is not recorded, but the success the family craved in their restless search would not be found through the move.

Florence, the eldest daughter (named for both of her grandmothers), was 16 years old by then. A young woman ready for adulthood, she had all the promise of a full and prosperous life ahead of her. However, that future hope was dashed when she died on 19 February 1900.[8] The death of one so young must have pitched her loved ones into an abyss of sorrow, but enough time to recover from the heartache was not available to them, as worse was yet to come.

By year's end, the loss of Florence was overshadowed by another bereavement. This time, the shock cut through to the very foundation of the family unit, as it was Elizabeth, the children's mother, whose life came to an end. She passed away from an agonising kidney disease on 9 November 1900. At just 47 years of age, she was gone, after a three-week illness.[9] Frank and the children must have been shattered by her loss!

The two older sons, William and James, now 19 and 17 years old, were making their own way in the world by then, but for Mary, not yet 11, and three-year-old John, the death of their mother while they were still so young was a tragedy that would leave an indelible imprint on their lives. Occurring at a time when they were still mourning the passing of their beloved older sister would have only added further complexity to their profound grief.

Their father now had to face up to a challenging dilemma. A mother taking care of the home and family while the father earned a wage for them all to live on was the traditional social arrangement, so losing the homemaker left the family in a very vulnerable position. Frank had to find a way to earn a living while providing them with adequate care at the same time. Failing in either of these areas meant risking government intervention and his children being placed in an orphanage or industrial school.

These Dickensian institutions were the only welfare options provided for children during that era, and the social view of the time was prejudiced against single fathers being capable of raising their children properly, so the threat of having his offspring taken from him against his wishes was real. A great deal of responsibility probably fell heavily onto young Mary's shoulders, but Frank would need a secure solution. Either to find employment that gave him the flexibility to keep his children with him while he did his job, or to locate a woman who would help him by taking care of them while he was working.

He may have managed to do that, as evidence suggests the possibility that he remarried a decade later.[10] Whatever he did to manage, it is clear that his plans for the future did not include his elderly mother-in-law, the children's grandmother and the only member of their extended family in the region.

Elizabeth's mother, Annie, had lived a long life. Already past the age of 80, she had faced many deaths. Her husband Thomas had gone 15 years before,[11] and like many women of the time, she had endured the harrowing ordeal of having to bury babes-in-arms as well.

While six of her nine children had lived into adulthood, both of her grown sons had perished as young men.[12] She and Thomas were then left with four daughters. The three older ones were far away in Bathurst and Parramatta, distances that would have seemed a world away to anyone at that time. Annie had never learnt to read or write, so without Elizabeth to do it for her, it is unlikely the thought of getting word to them even occurred to her. In so many ways and for so many reasons, Elizabeth would have been a precious lifeline to her mother. This daughter was some years younger than her older sisters, who were all close to each other in age.

Elizabeth had come along for Annie at a time when she was deep in grief over the loss of her older baby, Jane.[13] Caring for a new infant would have brought a focus that helped ease the sorrowing mother's heartache, assisting her in coming to terms with her loss. Elizabeth had been a great comfort from the very beginning, but where could her mother turn to, now that it was Elizabeth herself who had gone?

No evidence is available of how Annie became aware of the deaths in her family, but there is no doubt that the news would have been harrowing. The passing of the granddaughter would have brought great sorrow to the grandmother, who had watched her grow from a little girl to a young woman. With Elizabeth's death, she had lost more than a daughter. Just over a decade before, a homeless, pregnant Elizabeth with three young children to care for and a husband sent away to prison, had gone to her mother for help. Annie took her in, assisted her through her baby's birth, and continued to back her in keeping her children safe, until five years later when Elizabeth's mate returned to his family once more.

It is not hard to imagine such a shared history between the two women, forging a deep and solid bond between them. Now it was gone. So too was her child, her great comfort, her friend and companion. Such a loss must have been gut-wrenching for the old mother, squeezing the last bit of joy from her life. Daughter and granddaughter were both gone from her. Just how vulnerable the old Irishwoman had become without the availability of support from the women of her family would become all too apparent just two months later.

Ann was still on her own at Eulo. She must have been managing to make life work for herself, as she had been self-sufficient, from her family, for at least a year by that stage. It is unknown if she had any plans for the future. She may have intended to go on indefinitely as she was, or to eventually make her way back to family in New South Wales. Whatever ideas she may have harboured, all intentions were thwarted with an injury to one of her legs. What happened, or how serious the damage is, is not clear, but it seems to have been severe enough to curtail her independence. The traditional link for the elderly in that era was family, but that support was no longer available to Annie now that her daughter and eldest granddaughter were both gone. It is unlikely that her son-in-law, Frank, would have considered taking on what he would have seen as the added burden of the old woman in need of physical or medical help, to add to the pressure of providing a home and care for his two dependent children. For Annie, the only option was to appeal for State Government assistance. A doctor may have made the request on Annie's behalf, but the District Magistrate was the government official who had the power to take her into State care. There was only one place for him to send her: Dunwich Benevolent Asylum on North Stradbroke Island.[14]

The process of getting her there was complex. Transport needed to be arranged from outback Queensland to the Yungaba Immigration Centre on Main Street, South Brisbane, where she would be accommodated while waiting for the ferry.[15] Additional transport may have been needed to get her to the wharf as well, due to her injured leg. Even the passage from Eulo to the closest train link to Brisbane needed to be considered, as she would have to travel to Cunnamulla.[16] While details about Annie's journey are uncertain at this time, what is clear is the dramatic alteration in the landscape she would have encountered on her way eastward. The western region was her home for well over a decade, but her origins were in the east. Would the changing terrain remind her of past times? Would she take it all in enough to notice?

The broad, parched beauty of a weather-toughened landscape, beneath vibrant open skies, would eventually give way to open pasture lands, where cattle and sheep had easy grazing. Nutrient-rich soils holding life-giving moisture allowed food crops to be cultivated there as well. At that time of year, they would be ripening, ready to be harvested. Instead of the gnarly mulga scrub that hung on tenaciously in the thirsty earth, stands of tall, straight gums would be growing along flowing watercourses. Annie knew this kind of terrain from when she and Thomas moved to the western plains around Bathurst. That was where their long life together had come to an end. He remained sleeping still, while she had gone in search of a new life on her own.

Once she passed through the Great Dividing Range to reach the coastal plains, the landscape would have changed again. Here, nature was generous in her bounty. At that time of the year, creeks would be full to overflowing, as a result of drenching summer downpours. Vegetation would be green and lush, with crops ripe for the picking. In some instances, harvesting may have already been underway. The population was denser here as well. Such a contrast with the scarcely-settled world she had left behind.

Annie knew the productivity of this landscape made life easier here. It was similar to the land she had first

encountered on her arrival in the colony. When she initially
saw it, though, it felt alien and threatening. At that time,
she was Annie HART, a 17-year-old convict, scarcely out of
Dublin and alienated from all she saw.

Hesitant she may have been, but the rough city streets
she came from fitted her well for life in this strange new
world. Strong flexibility, feisty determination, and a sharp
wit were skills she had perfected. Annie would need them
to survive — and survive she did.

Later on, she combined her strengths with those of
another 'old lag", Thomas MAGEE, an exiled activist from
her homeland. The romantic rebel and the street-smart
pickpocket would have understood each other's secret ache
for home. In this wild, young land, they worked together to
create a new life, built a home together, and raised a family.
But now it was all gone. Once more, Annie was alone,
with not a soul to claim her. Brisbane's city streets, with
their frenetic bustling and buoyant vitality, were a strange
environment, so different to the dispersed population and
steady pace of the Queensland outback she was used to.
The optimism she saw everywhere must have been in stark
contrast to the anxiety she would have felt.

When she stepped onto the boat that morning, Annie
was once again revisiting her history. Earlier chapters are
repeated in the present. Some of the same, others bringing
variance. Water had brought her to this Grand Island, and
more than 67 years later, the element of water was playing
its part in her life once more. This time, it was taking her
away.

Once again, the official decree had sent her offshore
to an island unseen, to an uncertain future. Just as it
was back then, nobody stood on the shore to watch her
leave. But Annie knew there were people in her homeland
who would keep her memory alive and mourn her loss.
One of her earliest memories was the wail of the broken-
hearted, as wagons loaded with prisoners were taken from
Kilmainham Gaol to the transports. The surrounding
streets, filled with loved ones longing to say goodbye, would
erupt with a keening cry to make the angels weep. She
remembered how she felt when she was on that wagon. The

cry began within the walls, with those outside adding their voice as they realised the time had come.

When the enormous gates were pulled open, the wall of sound that hit her was as if the very stones were weeping. Passing under the five-serpent symbol above the gateway sent a chill down her very soul. She knew she would never see her home again. The unearthly sound of loved ones filling the world with sorrow told her that they could feel it too. The eerie cacophony travelled with Annie and her fellow prisoners as the cart trundled through Dublin to reach the city's edge. As the wagon of silent women passed, the residents of the city stopped to give voice to the common ache in their hearts at the sight. For many, these women brought others to mind; loved ones who had gone forever, too.

There was no shelter on the open cart, so the prisoners were at the mercy of the unpredictable spring weather. For days, they sat in the constant Irish drizzle, only to be relieved by the beating sun. They were tossed about on the back of the cart for the entire journey across the country to Cork City, adding to their sense of wretchedness. The wagon's struggle to negotiate the rough, rutted roads made the journey a gruelling ordeal for the poor women.

As they travelled, individuals and groups they passed reacted at the sight of them. Some stood still, in silence, but many raised their voices in the mournful keening wail. Ireland was losing her daughters, and deep in their souls, her people felt the harm of it.[15]

By way of contrast to that first leaving, Annie's departure from western Queensland had been unsung. Nobody was there to stand witness to her passing or to feel the pain of her absence. Sullen silence was the sound that marked her way through those grand plains. The yawning emptiness that held the bones of her loved ones in its dry, dusty embrace was the only presence. As Annie and her companions headed out into the open waters of Moreton Bay, screeching seagulls soaring on stiff coastal breezes raised the keening cry.

The smell of the briny sea would have reached her nostrils well before she encountered the bay. What was her response to the maritime triggers that hit her senses? The roiling roll of the boat as it cut through the waves? Did it stir her memories at all? The vigorous breezes, whitecap swells, or sunlight bouncing off the vivid blue sea?

Ann had experienced all these sights, sounds and sensations before. Back when the axis of her world had tilted, bringing a future she could not have foreseen. Did she hear the echoes whistling on the wind? Were there voices from her yesteryears calling her again? So many things are still the same. But then again, so many that were different. She had been one of 120 female convicts, from all parts of Ireland, who sailed on the morning tide from Cobh Harbour, aboard The Caroline. That was on 15 April 1833. Most of the women had never even seen the sea before, but were now heading out into the grand, wide ocean, on an epic and often terrifying voyage. The awesome power of the wind trapped behind the ship's great sails powered them on for 212 days, until they arrived at the other end of the Earth. Port Jackson must have felt so outlandish to them that they might just as well have landed on the moon!

Her marine passage this time was nowhere near as long. North Stradbroke Island was only 21 nautical miles (35 kilometres) from Brisbane. If all went according to plan, she would be delivered to her destination in about two hours. The wind was no longer applied to send her vessel sailing through the water. Now it was steam, the great marvel that powered the industrial age.

Once, she had youthful vigour as her ally to cope with journey's end, but now she was frail and worn down by the burdens of time. On this final leg of her protracted odyssey, the old woman must have yearned for her wandering to finally come to an end. What she saw when she arrived was a series of simple cabins dotted across the ridge above the wharf. What would she have made of the place? Would it have seemed like a refuge in an idyllic setting, or was there something austere in the atmosphere that warned her that the peace she sought could not be found here? Time has taken her responses from us, so the mind can only wonder.

When she disembarked, she stepped onto time-weathered boards that rested firmly on hulking great pillars. Men had put them there by their own brute force.

They had come to the island as unwilling workers, convicts, just as she had once been. Although long gone, the wharf and stone causeway that ran down to it stood in silent testament to the gruelling life they had endured here. It was just one of the many earlier uses the hamlet was put to, but it is no longer acknowledged.

When a frail old woman hobbled up the causeway that day, the staff would have seen nothing remarkable in her appearance, other than her leg, to perhaps mentally assess what sort of care she may require. To them, she was just another old pauper who had outlived her purpose. She would be housed and supervised in the same efficient manner that the 1,000 other occupants already here were being managed. Evidence of her life on the island is flimsy. One piece of paper is all that remains to give scant witness to her presence. Bare facts on a single sheet offer tiny clues, but convey nothing of the deep tapestry of life that was "Mrs Ann McGEE"*.

A shoddy recognition of a pioneer whose efforts helped forge the new nation that was, at that time, being celebrated.[16]

> *Cause of Admission: Bad leg ... Born: Southern Ireland ... daughter deceased ... Married: Windsor NSW to Thomas McGee — dead ... No money. No papers.*[17]

*Her surname was misspelt. The correct spelling is MAGEE.

Endnotes

1. Official registers record her name as Ann, but documents relating to members of her family name her Nora. Both are diminutives of the Irish name Honorah (pronounced *An-ora*), so that is probably her true name. Newspaper reports identify her as Annie, so she is given that name here, as it is assumed she was known by that name in society. However, Nora may have been what her husband and friends called her.

2. Elizabeth was born to Annie and her husband Thomas MAGEE, at Baulkham Hills in the Parramatta district of NSW, on 7 May 1852 (NSW BDM Vol 1854 1742 145). Fr J Coffrey, of the Parramatta Catholic Parish, Cumberland Shire, baptised her on 6 June of that year. (Vol 1852 742 69/1852 Reel 5025 Vol 68–70).

3. Frank was christened William Francis ADAMS. He was born in the Sydney district of NSW, to William ADAMS and Louisa ADAMS née TEASDELL, in 1851 (NSW BDM 250/1851 Vol 1851250 37A). Frank's mother died when he was six. His father perished late in 1877, the victim of a tragic drowning accident, at a property in the Seven Hills district of Parramatta. Whilst in a somnambulant state, he fell into the creek. His body was found the next day by his employer, who went searching for him after he had not arrived for breakfast.

4. Indications are that the couple's eldest son, William Francis Thomas ADAMS, remained in New South Wales. Born at Cobar, NSW, in 1881 (NSW BDM 12057/1881), he was about 16 years old by 1897. In that era, boys of

14 were considered old enough to work and earn a man's wage, so it is likely that he had been working for some time and had become independent from his parents. Leaving with them would have been unnecessary if he already had steady employment in the Bourke region. By the time of his death in 1970, he had relocated to Sydney. William's siblings were:

- James Joseph ADAMS, born 1883, Bourke district (NSW BDM 13175/1883). In 1897, about 14 years.
- Florence Louisa Ann ADAMS, born 1884, Brewarrina district (NSW BDM 15045/1884), about 13 years.
- Mary Leila May ADAMS, born 1889, Bourke district (NSW BDM 16107/1889), about eight years.

5. Frank had served seven years in prison for arson. The victim was a leading western NSW businessman, which would heighten Frank's notoriety, making it hard to turn his life around. With his parole complete, he had the freedom to leave the district and move to where his past was not as likely to follow him. Going to a new State would be the obvious choice.

6. John Henry ADAMS, born in Country Queensland in 1897 (QLD BDM 1897/C2354).

7. Dunwich Benevolent Asylum admission record gives a loose account of the family's movements during this time.

8. QLD BDM 1900 C1329. Ancestry.com 19 February 1900.

9. QLD BDM 1900 C1348. Elizabeth's death certificate records Bright's disease (a disease of the kidneys) as the cause of death. She died at her home in Miles Street, Jundah and was buried the next day (10 November 1900), at Jundah Cemetery (QLD Death Cert. 1900/1348 481), the same place her daughter was interred. (Find a Grave.com).

10. QLD Record of marriage 1911 C305 Mary Eliza LYONS and William Francis ADAMS. It is difficult to be certain that this was Frank without identifying the location. Locality data only separates Brisbane Metropolitan from Country QLD, so acquiring the certificate is the only way to know for sure. This is not being considered, as no extra data would be added to the story of Annie and her children. Frank's personal story became irrelevant once

Elizabeth died, and nothing would be revealed about the outcome for her children. There is also no relevance to the line of ancestry of interest to the researcher, that of Annie's eldest daughter, Mary Ann.

11. Annie's husband, Thomas MAGEE, died after a four-day illness, on 17 August 1885, at his eldest daughter Mary Ann's home, corner of George and Piper Streets, Bathurst. Despite being at least 80 years old, there was a quick deterioration, and it was likely unexpected, as no doctor had been called to attend him (NSW Death Cert. 1885/7212). He was buried the following day at the Bathurst Catholic Cemetery.

12. Thomas' death certificate lists three sons and two daughters who had preceded him. All three sons and one daughter have been accounted for, but at this stage, no record of the second girl child has been found. Their sons were:

   - John Joseph MAGEE was Ann and Thomas' youngest known child, born in the NSW Parramatta district, 1954 (NSW BDM Vol 1854353 71/1854 and Vol 18541922 145/1854). He died aged 24, of typhoid fever while working at Swallow Creek, Rock Forest in the Bathurst region of NSW and was interred at the Blayney Cemetery the following day (NSW Death Cert. 1878/4414).

   - Their older son, Thomas J. MAGEE, born 1848, Parramatta district NSW (NSW BDM 1410/1848 Vol 1848/1410 and 1012/1848 Vol 18481012 65), died in 1884. SMH Newspaper report said he died at the Cobb & Co. Hotel near Brewarrina, run by his brother-in-law Frank Adams (NSW BDM 7127/1884).

   - Ann's first child was also named Thomas. It is likely he died in 1841 before the age of two, when she and Thomas were living at Windsor, NSW. She would have been pregnant with Mary Ann at the time.

13. Jane MAGEE was Annie and Thomas' fourth daughter and probably sixth child. She was born in the Parramatta district in 1850 (NSW BDM Vol 18502072 67/1850 and 18501589 145/1850). Jane died in 1852 (NSW BDM

Vol 1852230 38B/1852), the same year and presumably before the time of Elizabeth's birth.

14. Dunwich Benevolent Asylum was the only institution available to house the poor and homeless. It operated for the entire state of Queensland.

15. http://www.kangaroopoint.com.au/history-of-kangaroo-point/

16. No record of how Ann travelled to the coast has been found to date. The railway had reached Cunnamulla in 1897, so that would have been the most convenient and cost-effective way for her to have travelled. Cobb & Co ran a coach between Eulo and Cunnamulla, so she is likely to have travelled that way. It is also unclear if she travelled alone or was given a chaperone. If she were alone, she would have had difficulty finding her way from the railway station to the accommodation on the southern side of the Brisbane River, as well as the Kangaroo Point docks. Further research may help clarify.

17. Information about transportation to the docks and transportation of women to Cork is among my earlier research. I will need to look for it and add it to the information.